The momen **dark eyes met ners, all those sharp edges snapped back into life as if they'd always been there.**

She didn't bother to hide the rounded shape of her belly as she stepped from the pool and walked over to where her clothes lay, discarded on the grass.

He watched her the whole time, saying nothing, filling the air with a complicated mixture of hunger and fury.

She sensed somehow that he wasn't going to break the silence, that he wanted her to do it. Well, if so, too bad. Maude sat on the grass to put her shoes on—slowly—and only once she had did she get to her feet and stand facing him, meeting his hot black stare. She didn't speak. She only raised an eyebrow. A thick, crackling silence filled the space between them.

"You're pregnant," he said at last, and Maude experienced a brief thrill at making him break first.

"Gosh, really?" she said dryly. "I had no idea."

His jaw hardened still further. He took a couple of steps toward her, then stopped. "It's mine."

Again, it wasn't a question.

A brand-new and thrilling quartet from
Harlequin Presents!

Work Wives to Billionaires' Wives

*Are you a billionaire in a bind? Call on the services
of Your Girl Friday!*

Your Girl Friday is the brainchild of Auggie, Maude,
Lynna and Irinka. Providing temporary personal
assistance to any billionaire in need, their company
is never short of work.

Probably because these savvy businesswomen,
best friends and committed "work wives" offer
world-class service with discretion guaranteed...
But in their latest Alpha billionaire bosses, could
they have finally met their matches? Both inside and
outside the boardroom!

PR expert Auggie is used to fixing problems. So
when billionaire boss Matias Balcazar needs saving
from a scandal tarnishing his reputation, her solution
is fake marriage. She's just not expecting him to
insist that *she* be the bride!

Billionaire's Bride Bargain by Millie Adams

Landscaper extraordinaire Maude has no problem
taming the grounds of ultra-rich Dominic's vast
estate. Taming her passion for the notorious playboy
himself is another question entirely! And their
spontaneous night together leaves her carrying a
scandal of her own...

Boss's Heir Demand by Jackie Ashenden

Both available now!

And look out for Lynna's and Irinka's stories from
Lorraine Hall and Caitlin Crews, coming soon!

BOSS'S HEIR DEMAND

JACKIE ASHENDEN

PRESENTS

Harlequin®
PRESENTS™

ISBN-13: 978-1-335-93955-5

Boss's Heir Demand

Copyright © 2025 by Jackie Ashenden

Recycling programs for this product may not exist in your area.

Harlequin Enterprises ULC
22 Adelaide St. West, 41st Floor
Toronto, Ontario M5H 4E3, Canada
www.Harlequin.com

Printed in Lithuania

MIX
Paper | Supporting responsible forestry
FSC® C021394

Jackie Ashenden writes dark, emotional stories with alpha heroes who've just gotten the world to their liking only to have it blown apart by their kick-ass heroines. She lives in Auckland, New Zealand, with her husband, the inimitable Dr. Jax, two kids and two rats. When she's not torturing alpha males and their gutsy heroines, she can be found drinking chocolate martinis, reading anything she can lay her hands on, wasting time on social media or being forced to go mountain biking with her husband. To keep up-to-date with Jackie's new releases and other news, sign up to her newsletter at jackieashenden.com.

Books by Jackie Ashenden

Harlequin Presents

The Maid the Greek Married
His Innocent Unwrapped in Iceland
A Vow to Redeem the Greek
Spanish Marriage Solution

Three Ruthless Kings

Wed for Their Royal Heir
Her Vow to Be His Desert Queen
Pregnant with Her Royal Boss's Baby

The Teras Wedding Challenge

Enemies at the Greek Altar

Scandalous Heirs

Italian Baby Shock
The Twins That Bind

Visit the Author Profile page
at Harlequin.com for more titles.

This one is for the real work wives, Maisey, Nicole and Megan. Love you guys.

CHAPTER ONE

DOMINIC LANCASTER LEANED BACK, placing one elbow negligently onto silk cushions of the Roman-style couch he was lolling on, and debated pouring himself more wine from the jug that sat on the low table near the couch.

Not that he needed any more wine since he'd already had a few goblets and was feeling perfectly pleasant. Then again, it was a *very* good French red and this *was* a bacchanal and he was the host. What kind of bacchanal would it be if the host himself didn't bacchanate?

Not that bacchanating was a word…but still, the point applied.

He held a bacchanal every year during midsummer, in the forest of his stately home, and it involved the usual—togas, masks, white silk pavilions in the forest, couches, grapes, wine—and then devolved into lots of sex.

People in his circle, the social elite of Europe, loved it and around the time the invites went out, the gossip columns were full of speculation as to who would be invited and who wouldn't, and why. It was a very select group.

There was no rhyme or reason to the invitations. Dominic chose guests purely on a whim, because there was nothing better than messing with people's heads, and he enjoyed the speculation and jockeying for position when invite season came around.

Tonight, though, was different, because he'd decided this would be the last bacchanal. Twenty years was long enough to retain ownership of his childhood home, and now was the time to get rid of it. Sell Darkfell Manor and the forest that surrounded it to anyone who would give him a good price, and then, with any luck, whoever bought it would raze the whole thing to the ground, thus saving him the bother of doing it himself.

Dominic surveyed forest from his couch, the white silk pavilion around him moving slightly in the night air. He'd had the pavilion put up to the side of the clearing and in the centre flamed a torch that leapt and flickered, casting strange shadows against the trunks of the ancient oaks.

More torches marked the paths that led to other small clearings, and other pavilions, all with couches and pillows, and wine and food. He could hear some of his guests laughing and shrieking, most of them already drunk.

A pity, really, to get rid of the forest—he'd had a lot of fun here after all—and maybe he could put a caveat on it or something. Or maybe not. Maybe it should go, along with the manor and everything else his father had touched.

Thoughts of his father never helped Dominic's mood and he was determined to enjoy himself tonight, so he leaned forward and poured more wine into the thick pottery goblet he only ever used for his bacchanals. Then he leaned back on the couch again, sipping at the wine.

Beyond the darkness of the trees came a squeal, which could only be Marissa. She was a lovely French socialite and Cannes regular, who'd begged him for an invite in various inventive ways, and she'd made it clear already that if he wanted to make it a night to remember she would be happy to oblige him. From the sounds of it, she was already occupied. Then again, it wouldn't be a bacchanal if he couldn't join in.

He sighed, wondering if, in fact, he could be bothered. He liked a good orgy as much as the next man, but sometimes it could be such a faff. Not to mention boring. It was nothing he hadn't done before, many times, and there were occasions where he couldn't see the point. Sexual pleasure was nice while it lasted but it was always so fleeting, and it had been years and years since he'd lost himself entirely in sex. That had been a young man's game, and he wasn't that young any more.

Besides, sex was also beginning to bore him. Parties were beginning to bore him. Even Lancaster Investments, the investment business he'd started around fifteen years ago, after he'd sold the last of his father's assets, was beginning to bore him. He had more money than he knew what to do with and when he sold Darkfell Manor, the last piece of his father's poisoned legacy would be gone and, after that, what challenges were left?

Dominic lay back on the couch and stared at the white silk above his head. He could go into space, or maybe buy a submarine. Or perhaps build a bunker in Iceland and retire there in solitary splendour. He could get himself a camel and ride off into the desert like Lawrence of Arabia, or maybe go exploring in the Amazon...

Really, the possibilities were endless.

At that moment Marissa squealed again and then came bursting through the trees on the far side of the clearing opposite him, laughing breathlessly as she came to a stop in front of Dominic's pavilion.

She wore nothing but a short white tunic and an owl mask, her long glossy black hair wild down her back, every bit of her long, golden body visible through the tunic.

A lovely woman.

Yet he wasn't moved. He'd seen her body before, knew everything it could do in bed and the sounds she made and the things she preferred. There was nothing about her sexually that he didn't know and nothing about the rest of her that interested him.

No one interested him, not these days.

So as she moved slowly and gracefully over to his couch, despite the flaring torchlight making her tunic seem half transparent, he remained...bored. He'd been bored for a long time, he suspected.

His lack of interest in her should have bothered him, but it didn't. In many ways, it was even a relief.

'Dominic,' Marissa purred in her sexy accent. 'I've been looking for you everywhere.'

'No, you haven't,' he said, surveying her as she walked over to his couch, hips swaying. 'I'm still here, where you last saw me.'

She laughed, stopping before his couch, her blue eyes

shining through the eyeholes of her mask. 'Have you been waiting for me?'

'Actually, I've been contemplating the mysteries of the universe.' He smiled, trying to muster up some enthusiasm, since this was last bacchanal and he'd told himself he should be having fun. 'Including the mysteries of the female gender.'

Marissa gave a little shiver—one of her trademark moves—then she reached for the small clasp on the shoulder of her tunic and undid it, letting the fabric flutter to the ground. 'Well, here I am,' she said softly, standing naked before him. 'You can contemplate me.'

Since she was right in front of him, he could hardly do anything else. She was beautiful, he couldn't argue with that. But he'd spent the last twenty-five years of his life contemplating the mysteries of the female gender and, as he'd already thought to himself, there was nothing about this particular example that intrigued him.

Perhaps that was why he felt bored.

There was no mystery in anything any more.

Dominic was an expert in the art of dissembling, yet Marissa must have picked up on his lack of interest, because she suddenly darted forward, leaning over him and brushing her mouth over his. Then she backed away, giving him a sultry smile. 'You can have me if you catch me.'

Then she turned and ran off naked into the forest.

Maude Braithwaite stood in the darkness, pressed against the trunk of one of Darkfell Forest's ancient oaks, and held her breath as the naked woman ran past her, barely a metre away.

The woman must not have seen Maude because she didn't pause, giggling as she disappeared into the darkness.

Maude let out the breath she'd been holding, shivering a little in her bare feet and nightgown. It wasn't exactly cold—it was midsummer—but it was still one in the morning and pitch black, so not quite warm either.

She'd been asleep in her little bedroom in the gamekeeper's cottage right on the edge of the forest, and had been woken abruptly out of a dream by the sound of someone screaming.

Tonight was the night of the Midsummer Bacchanal, and while she'd been told that the guests had been warned to keep away from the cottage, she supposed some of them hadn't followed the rules.

This was deeply annoying because, while hauling herself out of bed in the middle of the night to investigate wasn't mandatory, management of the forest was one of her responsibilities and she did want to make sure that her employer's rich friends hadn't accidentally set fire to something they shouldn't.

Maude was one of four women who ran Your Girl Friday, a company that offered speciality services to those rich enough to afford them, and her area of expertise was landscape design and forest management, anything to do with the natural world basically.

She loved nature, so when a groundskeeper contract for Darkfell Forest had come in, she'd jumped at the chance. Groundskeeper work had sounded intriguing, with the bonus of being responsible for the management of the forest. Her personal goal was rewilding a piece of land that her grandparents were going to leave her, and for that she needed, not only a touch more expertise, but also money. Handily, the contract she'd signed, which was for a year, paid exceptionally well.

However, what she had not loved was preparing a section of said forest for the bacchanal, since it involved turning a beautiful, wild place into what was essentially a party venue, i.e. making nature palatable for a whole bunch of rich people who didn't care.

It was always this dichotomy that bothered her while working for Your Girl Friday. Despising the rich and privileged, while also taking their money. She'd early on decided that money would go back to her rewilding project, and in return the people who employed her could stand to have a few lessons in caring for nature. Most of the time they were grateful, so she couldn't complain.

She was definitely going to complain about the drunken idiots currently cavorting around in these woods in the middle of the night, though. The forest wasn't inherently dangerous, but the fools could hurt themselves and someone had to make sure they were okay. That someone being her.

Anyway, she hadn't found anyone injured in the vicinity of the cottage, so she'd ventured a bit further into the forest itself, just to be certain.

She'd moved as many of the animals away from the bacchanal area as she could, but animals didn't obey human rules and one of them could have strayed somewhere it shouldn't and frightened someone. Not that she cared about humans. They could look after themselves. It was the animals she was concerned for.

The bacchanal was supposed to be a very private affair, with a specially curated guest list, and she'd been told—all the staff at Darkfell Manor had been told—that they shouldn't go into the forest while the bacchanal was being held. Maude hadn't wanted to anyway—she didn't care about bacchanals—and she'd been on the pointing of turning back to the cottage when the naked woman had run by her and she'd been forced into immobility.

The sound of the woman's progress gradually faded and Maude glanced back in the direction she'd come from to make sure no other naked people were in her immediate vicinity. Then she glanced back to the clearing beyond, where the torch flamed, causing dramatic shadows to leap and flare. A Roman-style couch had been placed artfully near the torch, beneath a pavilion of white silk, the curtains of which had been pulled back and held with jewelled ties.

A low table containing goblets, a bowl full of grapes, a jug of wine, and a platter of various finger foods had been placed near the couch, along with another low chair.

A man lolled indolently on the couch, on his back. He wore nothing but a white toga draped around a body that could have belonged to a Greek god, all hard, sculpted muscle and smooth tanned skin. A crown of golden laurel leaves rested in his hair.

He held a goblet in one large, long-fingered hand, the light of the flaring torch outlining the perfect lines of his face. Like his body, he was beautiful, but not in the way, say, Apollo or Hermes was beautiful. This man wasn't a boy. He was Zeus or Poseidon, or even Hades. An older god, stern, ruthless. Utterly masculine and completely in control of the universe he ruled.

Straight nose, long ink-black lashes, high cheekbones. There were lines around his eyes and his mouth, and through his short ink-black hair—from the severe widow's peak of his forehead all the way to the back of his head—ran a white stripe.

Maude's breath caught.

That stripe was famous. She didn't keep track of celebrity gossip and barely even checked social media. The world of humanity didn't interest her. Yet even so, that stripe marked him.

Dominic Lancaster, one of Europe's most notorious playboys, if not *the* most notorious. Owner of Darkfell Manor and the forest that surrounded it.

Also, her boss.

She'd never met him, only one of his assistants. She'd seen a few pictures of him—she didn't much care about the people she worked for, it was the landscape that mattered—but those pictures hadn't done him justice.

This was the first time she'd seen him in the flesh and…

Maude stared at him, transfixed.

If he'd picked up a thunderbolt and thrown it at her, she'd have let that bolt go straight through her.

It was baffling. She'd never felt that way about a man before.

She'd always been the odd one out, even with her closest friends, the other three of the Your Girl Friday team. Irinka, the team's secretary, who came from a Russian family and provided the rest of them with the connections they needed to the rich and powerful. Lynna, who was from Wales and had been raised in Greece, and who could make magic with food. And Augusta—known as Auggie—the sole American in the team, and who'd recently done a stint as a stewardess on a plane.

None of the others liked plants or forests the way she did. None of them liked communing with nature. And she knew they all considered her a little odd.

She was okay with that. She liked being odd.

She'd spent most of her early years in a Scottish commune with her mother, which had involved living very close to nature and not much in the way of schooling. Then her maternal grandparents, disturbed by the way she was being brought up, had forced her mother into giving Maude to them to raise. They'd tried to tame her with urban life, with concrete and rules and TV and homework instead of bonfires and storytelling and dancing.

Maude had found it tough, but eventually she'd managed to behave the way they'd wanted her to. Except for the fact that nature had got deep in her soul and now it was so much part of her, nothing could get it out.

It was nature that commanded her attention and, really, it was more normal for her to stop and stare like this at a tree, or a magnificent flowering shrub, than a man.

In the clearing, Dominic Lancaster put down his goblet and sat on the edge of the couch. Maude tensed. Perhaps he was going to run after the woman, in which case staying put was probably a good idea. She didn't particularly want him to find her creeping around in the forest, especially when she'd been told not to intrude.

He didn't move for a moment, the torchlight running over his skin and the carved lines of his torso revealed by the loose toga, bathing him in gold. Then he rose from the couch with a deliberate muscular grace that had Maude's heart racing, and walked slowly to where a white scrap of fabric lay in the leaf mould of the forest floor. Bending, he picked it up then continued over to where the woman had disappeared into the trees.

'You forgot something, sweetheart,' he called as he tossed the white fabric into the trees. 'You also forgot that I never run after a woman.'

A shiver ran unexpectedly over Maude's skin. His voice was deep and velvety and rich, with a darkness threading through it that seemed to connect with something inside her.

He stood very close and he was much taller than she'd expected. Much taller than she was. The crown of laurel leaves on his head, gleaming in the torchlight, and the way he held himself, as if he were indeed king of the gods, made her pulse begin to beat in a hard, insistent rhythm.

Men hadn't featured in her life. She hadn't met one she'd been even remotely attracted to and wasn't interested in meeting one. Men as a whole didn't interest her.

So this man, this complete stranger, shouldn't have warranted a second glance.

Yet she couldn't take her eyes off him.

She couldn't even take a breath.

He'd gone very still, as if he was listening, and Maude wouldn't have been surprised if it was her heart he'd heard thumping like a drum within the confines of her ribcage.

Something whispered in her brain, something dark and seductive, that was drawn to the man standing so close. A deep part of her that couldn't stop looking at the broad width of his shoulders and his powerful chest. That wanted her to run her hands across his olive skin, feel the prickle of crisp hair and then move further down, to the corrugated lines of his stomach left bare by the drape of the white fabric, the only thing that clothed him.

The forest bowed to him, the darkness in her head whispered. He was the king here. He was primal and raw, and if he wanted to chase a woman, she had no chance. He would bring her down onto the rich earth and take her, connect her so deeply to this forest and to him, she'd never escape.

There was an ache between Maude's thighs, an insistent ache she couldn't recall feeling so intensely before. She couldn't have moved if she'd wanted to.

'But you,' he murmured without turning his head, the velvety texture of his voice deepening. 'You, I might just make an exception for.'

He couldn't be talking to her, could he? No, it wasn't

possible. She was hidden in the shadows of the trees, in the darkness, he couldn't know she was there. In the forest, she was unseen. She was *always* unseen.

He's a god, remember? He could find you anywhere.

Her palms were damp, her heartbeat loud in her ears. She should melt into the trees and slip away, go back to bed. Pretend she hadn't seen him.

Yet…she didn't.

He turned his head slowly, looking in her direction. His face was shadowed, but somehow she could see the gleam of his eyes, black in the night. It wasn't possible for him to see in the dark, yet she was certain all at once that he knew she was there.

She had no idea how he knew, because she hadn't made a sound. Just as she knew that if she ran the way that other woman had, he would follow.

He would chase her through the forest until he caught her and then she would be his.

And he would be yours.

It came over her unexpectedly and very suddenly then, a wild thrilling rush of adrenaline, and before Maude was even conscious of doing so, she'd turned and had started to run.

CHAPTER TWO

It HAD ONLY been once he'd got to the edge of the clearing that Dominic had felt he was being watched. And it wasn't Marissa; he'd have to have been deaf not to hear her crashing through the undergrowth as she'd run from him.

No, someone else was watching him.

He'd stood there a moment after he'd thrown Marissa's tunic after her, having decided he couldn't be bothered to chase her, staring into the darkness, feeling the weight of someone else's gaze on him.

Then he'd caught a scent, earthy and musky and delicate, and very female, and abruptly everything male in him had sprung to instant life.

It was a sensual, deeply sexual scent, banishing his boredom, flicking switches inside him, turning on a current of pure electricity that he'd thought was long since dead.

It had been nearly fifteen years since he'd wanted anything. A long time since his life had been more than simply following a whim. Years since he'd taken his father's vast property development company and sold

JACKIE ASHENDEN   21

it off, piece by piece, netting himself huge profits and a sense of deep satisfaction.

He'd thought he'd come to the end of wanting anything, since whenever he had a hankering for something, he simply bought it or did it, letting nothing hold him back. He indulged himself at every opportunity, because why not?

Apparently, though, he hadn't come to the end of wanting after all, because someone had been watching him in the darkness, a woman, and every little piece of him had been intrigued.

He'd turned and stared into the shadows near an oak not far from where he stood, and though his night vision had been impaired by the light of the torch, he'd been able to make out a slender figure by the trunk of the tree.

A wood nymph.

There had been a second where he'd been sure he'd seen her eyes gleaming in the darkness, and an inexplicable need had risen up inside him. A primitive, basely masculine need, primeval almost.

So much so that when she'd turned and run, it had been instinct to run after her.

He'd told Marissa the truth. He never ran after a woman. He never ran after anyone. They all came to him and he liked it that way since it gave him all the power, and he liked power. Especially when he had it and other people didn't.

Which made his sudden mad dash after a woman he hadn't even laid eyes on completely inexplicable. Yet there was also an inevitability to it. As if she'd been in this forest for years, perhaps was even part of it, and had been waiting for him.

Waiting for him and him alone.

She made no sound as she ran, white fabric of her tunic or whatever she was wearing billowing out behind her, a pale figure in the night. Her bare feet hit the soft earth soundlessly as she dodged trees and leapt fallen logs, agile as a deer.

He felt strangely outside himself, as if he'd left Dominic Lancaster, renowned investor and notorious playboy, back in that clearing, and he were someone else now. A man with no past and no future, who was concerned only with the here and now. With the sound of his breathing, fast and hard, and the beat of his pulse, steady and strong. With the scent of the forest around him, spicy and dark, and the woman running ahead of him...

Thoughts gathered in his head, mundane thoughts. What was she wearing? All the guests wore either a white tunic or a toga and this was neither, and yet it was white, so maybe she'd styled it differently. Who was she? Why hadn't he noticed her earlier when he'd greeted everyone like the good host he was? He surely would have noticed her...

He pushed the thoughts aside. Those questions didn't matter. Nothing mattered. Nothing except running after her, a primitive hunter's instinct waking up inside him, pouring adrenaline through him. A wild excitement building inside him and an anticipation he hadn't felt for a long time, if he ever had.

He wasn't sure why he was feeling these things now, but he didn't question them. This was new, this was different. This made him feel as if he were sixteen again, and Craddock, the gamekeeper, had taken him deer hunting for the first time. He'd loved it, the thrill of the chase. Of course, he hadn't been able to shoot the deer when he and Craddock had finally tracked it down, and his father had sneered at what he'd deemed Dominic's 'softness'.

He wasn't soft now, though.

The forest around them thickened, becoming denser, which meant they'd moved out of the area he'd specified for the bacchanal, but he didn't care. The only thought in his head was to catch her, bring her down, so when the white fabric of her tunic caught on a branch and she slowed to release it, he put on a burst of speed and before she could free herself, he was there, catching her in his arms and pulling her hard against him, her back pressing against his front.

Her breathing was wild and her hair was in his face, a skein of raw silk that smelled just as delicious as she did. Christ, he'd never felt a woman as hot or as soft as she was.

She twisted in his grip, panting, but made no real effort to get away, nor did she speak. He bent his head, nuzzling against the side of her neck, her musky, feminine scent making him harder than he'd ever been in his entire life.

He didn't understand why he'd run after her, or why she was making him so hard, but, again, that didn't matter right now. What mattered was that she was in his arms and he wanted her. He wanted her more than he'd wanted anything in a very long time, and that was something to be savoured. He'd thought he'd lost the ability to feel anything more than mild pleasure and boredom, but clearly not.

'You were watching me, nymph,' he said, his voice rough and uneven. 'You think I didn't see you standing there in the darkness?'

Her breathing had slowed, and he could feel little trembles running through her, and for one timeless second they remained like that, her panting while he held her tight, his own breathing fast, inhaling the dizzying, intoxicating scent of her.

Then abruptly she turned in his arms and lifted her hands, her fingers in his hair, and she pulled his mouth down on hers.

And just like that Dominic lost his grip on reality.

Everything slid away. His father. His company. His guests. His party. There was only the forest, dark and still around him, and the woman in his arms. Her mouth, hot and hungry, and the taste of her igniting something in him he'd thought long dead. Something desperate and raw.

He slid his fingers into the silken warmth of her hair and closed them into fists, gripping her, holding her still as he devoured her, pushing his tongue into her mouth and exploring her heat and her taste. So sweet and yet with a tart edge that excited him, that made him want to kiss her deeper, harder.

She made an animal sound, throaty and husky, and it wasn't in protest. Not when her hands were on his bare chest, running over his skin, her nails scratching him as she reached down over his stomach and further down. He wore nothing but his toga and a growl escaped him as her fingers found the achingly hard length of his shaft and closed around it.

The touch was too much. He wanted to get rid of this excess fabric between them, have her skin next to his. He wanted to taste her. Lick her. Bite her. And only then, once he'd had his fill, would he give her what she so clearly wanted.

She didn't make a sound as he took her down onto the forest floor, onto a pile of bracken that God himself couldn't have positioned any better, and then he was casting his toga to the side before tackling whatever it was that she was wearing, tearing it straight down the middle and off. She reached for him as he pulled it away from her, hungry in the night, but he took her hands and pinned them above her head with one hand, while with the other he began to map her body hidden in the darkness.

She was delicate and slender, yet the curve of her breast fitted his palm to perfection and her skin was warm silk. She moaned as he brushed his thumb over her hard nipple and then gasped as he slid his hand lower, to her hip, fingertips lightly brushing over it, touching the side of one thigh, then exploring between them. She shuddered, her sharp intake of breath loud in the night air, as his fingers found damp curls and slick, hot skin.

She smelled like sex and the forest itself, and he found himself raising his fingers to his mouth and licking her flavour from them. A flood of intense hunger swept through him, drowning the last remaining piece of Dominic Lancaster, and now there was only him. Only the trees. Only her. Female to his male. Raw and primeval as the forest itself.

He released her hands, but only to grip her thighs and spread them wide. Then, pinning her hips in place, he bent and began to devour her like the beast he'd become.

Maude lay on her back, conscious of nothing but the feel of his strong hands holding her pinned to the bed of soft bracken, his hot mouth between her thighs. Of his tongue exploring her delicately and yet with an insistence that made her tremble. And of the sharp, agonising pleasure, winding tighter and tighter.

It was a mystery how she'd ended up here. Why she'd run from him instead of calmly walking out from behind the tree and telling him who she was, before going off to her cottage alone. Why she'd kept running through the forest, filled with a totally alien and yet wild exhilaration, part of which was delicious fear and yet another part excitement.

Something sensual had awoken within her as she'd run headlong into the dark, an awareness that had seemed to saturate the forest around her. An awareness too of the man pursuing her.

He might have said he didn't run after a woman, yet he'd run after her, somehow staying close behind her even though a man of his size and power shouldn't have been able to run as fast or know the forest as well as she did.

When the branch had caught her nightgown a simple rip would have pulled it free. She hadn't needed to slow down, yet she had. Maybe she'd slowed deliberately. Maybe a deep part of her had wanted to be caught. Wanted *him* to catch her. Not just any man, but him.

Zeus, the king of the gods.

The god of the forest.

He *had* caught her then, his arms closing around her, pulling her back against him. All the breath had gone out of her, all her awareness captured by the male body behind hers and the power of his arms banded about her. The heat of him had been incredible and he'd felt so hard, like rock, and so tall. He'd towered over her, like one of the trees she'd been hiding next to.

There was no hiding from him, though.

He was a god.

Now, she stared up into the darkness of the tree canopy, seeing nothing but stars as he lay between her thighs and did something wicked with his tongue, causing everything to light up inside her, making her feel like one of those torches, flaming in the night.

She cried out, shaking as the pleasure crashed through her, and she was still trembling with the aftershocks when he rose from between her thighs and stretched himself out above her. His toga was long gone, but the laurel leaves in his hair were still there, gold gleaming against stark black and that snowy white stripe.

What are you doing? He's your boss. You don't even know him.

The thought was dim, the sound of it reminding her of her grandmother and all the rules she'd been given. Rules she'd had to follow if she wanted to stay with them and, since she'd had nowhere else to go, she'd stayed. And followed their rules. But she was tired of that. Tired of rules.

So what if he was her boss? So what if he was a stranger? He was part of the forest and she was too, and she didn't care what she should and shouldn't do. She'd never been in a man's arms before, never wanted to be, but this felt right. This felt primordial and so was she.

A current of intense sensual awareness ran through her, making her conscious of her own sexuality in a way she'd never been conscious of before. Of how right this was and how natural to come to full awareness of herself as a woman right here on the forest floor, beneath the trees she loved. With a man who seemed part of the forest himself.

He was above her now and he smelled so good, warm and earthy and spicy. Somehow familiar and yet intoxicating. Sexual. Carnal.

He lowered his head, his teeth at the side of her neck, and he bit her like an animal, making her shudder, waking pleasure inside her yet again. Then she felt the touch of his tongue against her skin, as if he was tasting her the way he had between her thighs, and another rush of heat flooded her, prickling over her entire body.

Obeying an instinct that came from deep inside her,

Maude lifted her arms to him, pulling his big, power-ful, muscular body down on hers, finding his mouth and kissing him with wild abandon. She tasted herself on his lips and that was as it should be. Right. Power-ful. *She* felt powerful, the primal feminine to his mas-culine, a goddess in her own right and now demanding his surrender, as she'd given him hers.

She had no idea what she was doing, but she didn't care. Tonight there were only the rules she made her-self and if this kiss involved sharp teeth and tongues, then it did. They were animals tonight, connecting in their purest form.

He made a low, guttural sound as she bit his bottom lip and then his hands were in fists in her hair, holding her still as he kissed her back with raw savagery, nip-ping, biting, licking, tasting.

She moaned, her hands pressed against the velvety skin of his chest, all heat and the prickle of hair as she touched him. He was naked but for the crown of laurel leaves and he was magnificent, and even though the darkness hid most of him, his crown deemed king in this forest.

Tonight, she would be his queen.

He shifted his hips and without hesitation pushed in-side her, hard and deep, and it felt right to wrap her legs around his waist and arch beneath him, making him slide even deeper. Sensation rushed through her as she felt herself stretch around him and tighten, holding him inside her. Glorious pleasure with a slight edge of pain to make it sweeter.

She groaned, inner muscles tightening around him, and then his mouth was on hers again, the kiss savage, passionate, wild. He moved, inevitable as the turn of the earth, as the change of the seasons, the rise of the sun and the fall of night.

There had always been this darkness inside her, a hint of primitive savagery that she hadn't wanted to uncover. But now she did. Now she went deep into that darkness and found him there waiting for her.

He moved faster, harder, and she moved with him, the forest surrounding them, glittering with the wild magic they were generating between them.

And it was magic. It was glory. It was a connection she'd never dreamed she'd ever have, but it was happening right now and she was losing herself to it. Losing herself to the pleasure and the night.

When the orgasm came for them both, it blazed hot through each of them, leaving them flaming in the dark. Both, like torches.

Dominic opened his eyes to find himself lying on his back in the middle of the forest, completely naked. Dawn was filtering down through the forest canopy above his head, dew chilling his skin.

For a moment he had no idea where he was or why he was lying naked in a forest. He felt…relaxed. Which he shouldn't have considering the location, and yet, he did. Alcohol and other such…substances, didn't usually leave him feeling so boneless and sated, though they were usually the reason he woke up somewhere he didn't expect.

But he wasn't hungover or anything else. In fact, he felt oddly energised.

He sat up at the same time as a beam of sunlight shone through the trees, falling on his skin like a benediction, and that too felt good, so he stayed there for long seconds, enjoying the feeling of sun on his skin.

Then memory began to filter through, of the darkness and warm skin, of breathless cries and intense pleasure...

Abruptly, he looked around for the woman he'd spent all night having sex with like an animal in the dark, but there was no sign of her.

He was alone.

Damn.

He'd never had a woman like her in all his life and he'd had more women than he could count. All beautiful. All skilled lovers. All ready to do whatever he wanted.

But *that* woman... She'd been all passion. All heat. Fire between his hands. She'd taken what she'd wanted from him, no holding back, matching him passion for passion. He'd taken too and she'd let him just as he'd let her. She hadn't asked him what he wanted or watched him to make sure he was enjoying himself or watched herself to make sure she only looked sexy. She hadn't cared. It had been dark, admittedly, so neither of them had been able to see, but she hadn't teased him or taunted him, or tried in any way to engage him. No, she'd used him, he suspected. Taken what she wanted as if she owned him.

And he'd found himself giving as good as he got, his reward her cries of pleasure, her nails digging into his back, her teeth against his shoulder.

They hadn't spoken. They'd let their bodies speak instead and it had been…

He let out a breath, closed his eyes, and tilted his head back, feeling the warmth of the rising sun on his face.

He felt…bloody amazing. His body sated. His mind at peace.

That hadn't happened in years.

The pursuit of pleasure had always been one of his interests, and he hadn't cared where it came from. The urge to fill the gaping void inside him with sensation. It was always there that void, or maybe it wasn't a void. Maybe he was just dead inside and sex and pleasure were the defibrillator he used to jump-start what was left of his soul.

In which case, the sex he'd had last night had been one hell of a charge. He could feel it still, passion burning in the depths of him, embers of a fire that had ignited the night before and were smouldering away still.

Who was she?

It didn't matter. What mattered was something coming alive inside him as he'd run through the forest in the dark, an exhilaration, an excitement. The instinct of a hunter, chasing sensual prey.

He'd never felt it before, not at any of the bacchanals he'd held in years gone by, and some of them had been good. But this…this was something else. This was what a bacchanal was *really* about, wild, savage, carnal.

He'd taken her down to the forest floor and when he'd pushed inside her, he'd felt as if he'd come home almost.

Christ.

He could go over the guest list again and find out who she was, but there had been something magical, mystical even, about not knowing. As if finding out who she was would break a spell.

Fanciful even for him, but perhaps it was best if what happened at the bacchanal stayed at the bacchanal. After all, he knew how passion played out. Eventually it died, no mysteries left, and cue the boredom.

He didn't want that to happen.

Dominic sighed again, took a deep breath of the dawn air, then pushed himself to his feet. His ridiculous laurel crown had come off at some point in the night and he found it under a fern. He picked it up, settled it on his head, found his toga and threw it over his shoulder. Then, not far from the bed of bracken he and the nymph had slept on the night before, he found the remains of more white fabric. It was not one of the togas or tunics that had been issued to the guests.

It was a white nightgown. And was ripped right down the front.

Which meant only one thing.

The woman he'd spent the night with in the forest had not been one of his guests at all.

CHAPTER THREE

MAUDE PAUSED A moment along the forest path that ran up the side of the hill and took a breath. It wasn't steep, but she'd experienced a distinct lack of energy for the past couple of weeks and it was annoying. She'd be turning over earth, or raking leaves, or doing any one of the thousand tasks involved in managing the grounds of Darkfell Manor, and she'd suddenly find herself needing a lie-down.

Normally, she was fit and had boundless energy, so it was puzzling.

Or rather, it wasn't puzzling, not if she really thought about it, but she didn't want to think about it, and so puzzling it remained.

Nothing at all to do with the wild night in the forest five months earlier, where she'd lain in the bracken with the god of the forest.

Thankfully she'd woken up before he had, long before dawn, and had hurried back to the groundskeeper's cottage. She hadn't wanted to shower the scent of him from her skin, but her feet had been dirty and she'd been cold, so she'd stepped under the warm water and let it do its work.

Afterwards she'd stood in front of the mirror in the tiny bathroom, gently touching the marks he'd left on her body, her only proof that it had actually happened. She'd let her boss, a stranger, run after her in the woods and she'd let him catch her. Let him take her to the ground and have her.

A reminder that, for one night, she'd been wild.

Her grandparents would be appalled if they knew, but she'd thought then that with any luck they'd never find out.

Unfortunately for her, though, luck wasn't her side.

It had been six weeks after her last period that shc'd eventually taken herself off to see the doctor in the little village twenty miles from Darkfell. The doctor had given her the news she'd dreaded, along with various pamphlets and instructions on what to do next, and Maude had decided that the question about what *exactly* she was going to do wasn't one she could answer just yet.

Sonya, her mother, was still in the Earthsong commune, in Scotland, and that was off grid, so she was uncontactable. Not that she wanted to contact her mother, since her mother hadn't bothered staying in contact with her after her grandparents had taken her away. Even apart from that, there was also the fact that Sonya didn't know what to do with a baby, especially when she hadn't wanted the one she'd had.

Maude couldn't talk to her grandparents about it either. They'd ask too many question about the baby's father, and the truth wasn't something she could tell them, not if she wanted the piece of land they were going to leave to her. They'd always been very clear that they didn't want her going down the same path as her mother had.

There were the other Your Girl Friday girls, but although they were her closest friends—they'd all been to university together—Maude felt weird about telling them. They wouldn't be judgmental, but they'd be worried and she couldn't bear the pressure of their concern.

Really, if she told nobody, then maybe she wouldn't actually be pregnant?

Don't be stupid. The doctor told you that you are.

Maude sucked in a breath of the rich, forest-scented air and continued her trudge up to the small picturesque waterfall that emptied into a perfect small pool. The waterfall was surrounded by trees and it was peaceful. Grasses and wildflowers grew around it and Maude would often bring her lunch up there for an impromptu picnic whenever she wanted to sit and think.

It was hot for early autumn, and even with the slight bite in the air, Maude was sweating by the time she got to the top of the hill.

Soon she'd be twelve weeks. Soon she'd have to admit to the reality of this baby and, since she hadn't made a decision earlier, soon she'd have to decide what she was going to do about it.

And him? What about him?

Despite the heat, she shivered.

She couldn't tell him. After that night, he hadn't returned to Darkfell, and she hadn't asked about him. There was limited Internet at the manor and none at all in the groundskeeper's cottage, so she was able to dismiss him from her thoughts entirely. Out of sight, out of mind.

But she couldn't keep telling herself that for ever.

Maude sat down at the side of the lake and dipped a finger in the water. It was cold, deliciously so, but not too icy for a swim.

She hadn't brought her bathing things—she'd intended to come here for some peace to decide what to do about the baby—but the waterfall and pool were very isolated, and no one except Mr and Mrs Harris, who managed the manor, were in residence, so the chances of someone seeing her were just about zero.

Still, she gave a cursory look around at the surrounding woods to make sure she was completely alone, then she kicked off her worn boots before stripping off her muddy jeans, T-shirt, and underwear. Then, standing naked by the pool, she glanced down at the small rounded bump of her stomach.

Her child, conceived on the floor of Darkfell Forest. She touched her stomach gently, and allowed herself to finally think about her baby.

He or she was a gift from the forest and they belonged here with it, she felt that suddenly and quite strongly.

Child of the man who owns the forest, too.

That was true, but what little she did know of Dominic Lancaster was that he wasn't a family kind of man. After that night, she'd indulged herself once he and all the guests had left, taking advantage of the manor's Internet and doing a few Internet searches on her laptop.

There were gossip sites and discussion threads dedicated to his sensual exploits, with numerous pictures and videos of parties and clubs he'd attended, and in every single one of those videos and pictures the charisma he gave off was so palpable it mesmerised her.

She'd touched those powerful shoulders. She'd kissed his beautiful, hard mouth. She'd had him inside her...

Now his child is inside you too.

A thick, hot feeling gathered in her throat. She'd really tried to be what her grandparents had wanted. Hardworking, honest. Reliable. Thinking through her actions before she made them and being alert to the consequences. She'd never been a rebellious teen, since her grandparents had made it very clear that they wouldn't put up with what they termed 'any nonsense'. They hadn't wanted her to turn out like her mother, who'd left home at sixteen after falling pregnant to a much older man and then running off to join the Earthsong commune.

Sonya had been wild, reckless, and could never be told what to do. She'd also been distracted and impatient, and had preferred socialising to parenting and Maude had often ended up being looked after by other people in the commune.

Maude's grandparents had put up with what they saw as their daughter's irresponsibility for ten years before finally coming to Earthsong and taking Maude away permanently.

She didn't like to think about that day, because she'd loved the commune. She'd loved not going to school, loved one of the older ladies who'd managed the commune's garden and who'd let Maude play there all day if she'd wanted to. She loved her wild, reckless mother too.

But Sonya hadn't loved Maude enough to keep her. She'd let her parents take Maude away with only a shrug. Then she'd cut off contact with them and Maude without explanation. Permanently.

After that, Maude had often felt untethered as a child. As if she'd lost an anchor and the current had been dragging her and she'd had nothing to hold onto. She'd had no real home to go to, no place where she'd felt she belonged. She'd tried to fit in all through the rest of her childhood and into adulthood, had tried to find her place in the world. But the only place that had felt like home was the forest, and Darkfell Forest in particular.

She didn't want to leave, didn't want to give up her job, but it was a fixed-term contract and maternity leave wasn't part of it.

Gran would have told her that it was her own stupid fault and she should have known better. That she had too much of her mother in her, and did she really want to waste her life the way Sonya had?

Now, the thick, hot feeling in her throat tightened and her eyes prickled, but she forced the feelings away. Hard.

Having a baby *wasn't* a waste of her life and she *wasn't* going to leave, either. This child was part of the forest and she couldn't think of a better place for it to be than with her, here in Darkfell. Maybe she could manage things with her job so she could stay with the baby.

No, there was no maybe about it. That was exactly what she was going to do, and she'd fight tooth and nail to make that happen.

Braced by that thought, she bent down and picked a wildflower, weaving the stem into her hair on a whim. Then she picked another and another, weaving more flowers into her hair as she went, covering herself with parts of the forest.

She was going to have to tell people, she knew that.

First her friends, then... Well, maybe just her friends for the moment. The one thing she certainly wasn't going to do was tell Dominic Lancaster.

Picking a couple of forget-me-nots, she wound them into her hair beside each ear, then picked her way around the lake to the rocks where the waterfall splashed down. It was only a little waterfall and not very powerful, delightful to stand beneath and let the water wash over her like an outdoor shower.

She tilted her head back and closed her eyes, letting the gentle pressure of the water ease away the tight knot of fear that had settled in her chest. Letting the calm of the forest enter her soul and soothe it.

After a couple of minutes she turned and dived cleanly into the pool. Arrowing down to the sandy bottom, she touched it lightly, a little ritual of greeting to the spirit of the pool and waterfall, then pushed herself back up to the surface. Then she turned onto her back and closed her eyes, floating for a time, letting her mind settle.

Then Maude slowly became aware that she wasn't alone. Someone was standing in the trees beside the lake, watching her.

A very tall, powerfully built man, with a white stripe running through his black hair.

Dominic wasn't sure how long he'd stood there watching the woman. He'd been in the forest, showing a developer currently interested in the property around, and had been intending to show him the waterfall and the pool, but as they'd approached, he'd caught a glimpse of bare skin and long golden hair and had quickly decided the developer should return to the manor without him.

Obviously, he hadn't gone too, since if there was a naked woman bathing in his pool, he wanted to know exactly who she was and why she was there.

Not that he needed to ask her, since the knowledge had been sitting in his subconscious for months now, and had since become part of him.

There was only one woman it could possibly be and that was the beautiful wood nymph he'd caught in the forest on his last bacchanal. And of course it was her. He hadn't seen her face, hadn't spoken to her, knew her only by her scent, the soft sound of her cries, and the silken heat of her skin, but it was her all the same.

He knew it like he knew his own name.

He'd watched her turn her face to the waterfall as it cascaded over a delicately curved body, with honey-gold skin, and then he'd watched her dive gracefully into the pool before rising onto the surface and rolling onto her back.

Wildflowers were tangled in hair the colour of ripe wheat and caramel, long tresses like golden kelp fanning around her head as she floated in the water. Her body was framed beautifully, high, rounded breasts with pretty pink nipples, the curve of hip and thigh proportioned with perfection. A slender woman, yet he remembered the way she'd felt, delicate but with a subtle strength in the arms that had wrapped around him and in the thighs that had closed around his hips.

He felt like a voyeur watching her now, but he didn't move. His scruples had always been few and scant enough that he couldn't bear to drag himself away. She was a beautiful wood nymph crowned in wildflowers, and she was bathing in his pool.

Abruptly, as if sensing she was being watched, she rolled onto her front, the water splashing as her head turned in his direction and her gaze met his. She had warm brown eyes, flecked with the same gold as her hair. They made his heart feel as if it had missed a beat.

Her mouth opened and her eyes went wide with surprise, and she submerged herself to her shoulders in the water, obviously trying to hide herself.

He should have looked away. He really should, but he'd never been a gentleman, not once, and why shouldn't he look anyway? The darkness had hidden her that night in the forest, but now the sun was shining and she was naked, and he couldn't tear his gaze away.

'Hello, nymph,' he said. 'What are you doing in my pool?'

Her features were as delicate as the rest of her, small and precise, with a full mouth and high cheekbones, and slightly winged dark gold brows. An ethereal beauty, almost otherworldly, and subtle enough that he might not have noticed it in another context. But right here, right now, it was all he could see. Those gold-flecked eyes of hers held a strength and a fire that caught his interest and held it.

'I'm swimming,' she said. 'What does it look like?'

Her voice held a husk to it that went straight to his groin, but her tone was decidedly un-nymphlike. Which also went to his groin. He'd always liked a woman with spirit.

'You appear to have forgotten your bathing suit,' he pointed out. 'Did you perhaps think you could hire one? Alas, neither this pool nor the manor are open to the public.'

'I'm not the public.' She eyed him with deep suspicion. 'I work here.'

That gave him pause. She worked here? It was possible, he supposed. He had many houses dotted all over the globe, most of them fully staffed, and he didn't know the names of all those staff. But he did know the names of the Darkfell staff. They'd been there since he was a child. John and Polly Harris. Those were the only two. Except…

John had been getting on in years and had told Dominic that he should hire a gardener and someone to do forest upkeep, so Dominic had instructed John to employ whomever he thought best. Dominic trusted his judgement. But this…sprite could *not* be the person John had hired, surely?

She couldn't be the woman in the woods that night either, right?

Dominic wasn't often surprised, but he could feel shock working its way through his body now.

He'd found that nightgown the next morning, but he hadn't bothered finding the owner. In fact, he'd put it out of his mind. Yet every now and then he'd find himself looking over the guest list of that last bacchanal, studying the names of the female guests and wondering.

It hadn't been any of them, he was sure, which meant he should keep looking. Because if that woman hadn't been a guest then perhaps he'd involved someone else, someone unsuspecting who hadn't known what was happening. Then again, she hadn't protested, hadn't pushed him away. When he'd caught her, she'd kissed him just as savagely as he'd kissed her. There had been nothing reluctant about her, nothing at all.

She was staring at him now, her gaze wary, her shoulders still underwater.

'Please tell me,' he said, 'that it wasn't you that night.'

She flushed. 'What night?'

'You know what I'm talking about.'

'I don't.' She glanced away, her chin jutting at a mutinous angle. 'It's cold. I need to get out. Which means you need to bugger off.'

He decided to ignore that. 'You're John's hire, aren't you? From that agency. You're the gardener.'

She glanced back again, her jaw tight. 'I prefer groundskeeper. Since I also look after the forest, not just the garden.'

Hell. It *had* to have been her, in that case. There was no other possibility. As the thought hit him, a shock of sexual desire pierced him, so intense it took his breath away, and for a moment he had to fight to get it under control. Which hadn't happened for twenty years. In fact, he couldn't remember the last time he'd been in the grip of such intense sexual hunger.

He'd spent the last fifteen years indulging his appetites shamelessly, letting himself have whatever he wanted, and why not? He deserved it after the long battle first to gain control of his father's company, then to break it up piece by piece. After the years of his childhood where everything had come with a price, with strings. Short strings, long strings, but *always* strings. Everything had been a negotiation, a deal. Everything a quid pro quo. His father had taught him to be ruthless and hard when it came to getting what he wanted, to negotiation, and, since it was the only power he'd ever had as a child, he'd learned.

He'd learned to control his emotions too, to not let need or desire get in the way of getting the best deal possible. Of course, now he'd achieved what he wanted, he'd lengthened the leash he kept on his appetites, seeing no point in not indulging them. But he never let them get too out of control, never let them control him. He remained in command of himself always.

Except apparently he hadn't with this woman. Who, despite having been under him for one whole night, made him want to have her again. And again, and again...

Dominic knew he should walk away. Should turn and go back to the manor, sign the papers that would sell this godforsaken property, and leave without a backward glance, never to return.

But he didn't.

Instead, he strolled over to the edge of the pool and looked down at the woman in it, her hair a golden veil around her face, the remains of wildflowers, blue and pink and purple, still caught in the wet strands.

She stared back, the gold flecks in her eyes glittering with temper.

'It was you,' he said, and he didn't make it a question this time. 'That night in the forest.'

She gave him an aggravated look. 'Can you please go away? It's cold and I want to get out.'

But he was in a position of power now, his favourite position, and he was finding it far too satisfying getting under her skin. She'd turned him inside out that night and apparently still had magic enough to do the same thing now, and what was sauce for the goose was good for the gander, et cetera.

So he merely folded his arms and remained where he stood. 'Then by all means get out. Don't let me stop you.'

The golden sparks in her eyes glittered brighter, and again he felt that delicious rush of excitement and anticipation. It would be glorious if she got out, only to run again, naked and dripping wet. He'd run too, and this time he'd make sure to catch her sooner, so that they could get to the pleasurable part quicker, her mouth on his, all raw heat and honey, with a sharp edge.

He hadn't had a woman since that night. He'd been busy with a new startup in LA and had told himself he hadn't had the time to find a new lover. Lies, of course. He'd had the time, he just hadn't had the inclination, and now two months of celibacy were starting to bite.

That had to be the reason he felt this way. The *only* reason. If she didn't get out, it didn't matter to him. He'd find someone else to lose himself in…wouldn't he?

You want her, though.

She was staring at him furiously from the water, and, yes, he had to be honest with himself. He wanted her. He wanted her badly.

'I can stand here all day,' he murmured. 'You, on the other hand…'

'Bastard,' she muttered, shooting daggers at him.

Oh, she had spirit. He liked that *very* much. 'I'm your boss. I could fire you for that.'

'Fine. Fire me. Now go the bloody hell away.'

'I've touched every inch of your body. What does it matter if I see it?'

'This is sexual harassment.'

'Take it up with HR.'

Her full mouth compressed. If looks could kill, his broken body would be floating in the water next to her.

What are you doing? You're usually much better with women than this.

It was true. Then again, he liked power games, and the pettier the better, especially with women who were as fiery and stubborn as this one.

Still, making her sit in cold water to gratify his need to win was perhaps too petty, even for him. He really should turn around and let her get out, and then they could have a proper conversation.

The water of the pool was clear and as he prepared to turn around, he could see the pale shape of her body beneath the surface. She had her arms crossed protectively over her chest, and maybe it was a distortion of the water but it seemed as if her stomach was…

A shaft of ice pierced him and he took a step closer to the edge of the pool before he could stop himself. 'Get out,' he ordered.

People always did what he told them when he used that tone of voice, and this woman was no different. Her eyes widened and she'd already half risen out of the pool before she realised what she was doing, brown eyes flashing with anger as she sat again.

But it had been enough for Dominic.

Enough to see the water glistening on the bare skin of her belly, revealing the small, rounded bump of early pregnancy.

Dominic met her gaze, every inch of him suddenly

burning with a fury he hadn't thought was possible for him to feel these days.

'Get out of the water,' he said coldly. 'Get out of the water *now*.'

CHAPTER FOUR

MAUDE EYED HIM WARILY, her heart beating far too fast
and far too hard.

He stood by the edge of the pool, his arms crossed
over his broad chest, every line of his tall, powerful figure drawn tight with anger. It burned in eyes dark as the
night too, turned his beautiful mouth hard, and made a
muscle leap in his strong jaw.

He was dressed casually, in faded jeans that sat low
on his hips and did wonderful things to his thighs, and
a simple black T-shirt that clung to his muscled chest.
The clothes should have made him less intimidating,
but somehow they only highlighted it.

Dominic Lancaster. Her boss. Her god of the forest.

The father of her baby.

A baby she'd thought he'd never know about...at least
until now.

The moment she'd locked eyes with him as she'd
floated in the pool, she'd known she wasn't going to get
out of this with her secret intact. Not given how the tension that had been there that night in the forest had suddenly leapt between them again, electric and resonant.

She'd tried to stay beneath the water as he'd strolled to the edge of the pool, but his dark gaze had seen too much. She should have pretended she was a lost tourist and not given away the truth that she was his employee, but he'd surprised her. She'd been surprised too by her own reaction to him. It had been months since that night in the woods, yet the moment she'd made eye contact with him, she'd felt as if she couldn't breathe.

She knew she shouldn't have got angry with him. She knew she shouldn't have called him a bastard. Her grandmother had instilled in her the importance of being polite to people and calling him a bastard wasn't at all polite. But, God, the way he looked at her made her skin feel so tight she wanted to crawl right out of it.

And that wasn't even counting the secret she was trying to hide from him. The secret curled up in her belly that she desperately hoped he hadn't noticed.

Clearly she'd hoped in vain. He must have seen her stomach when she'd half stood in instinctive obedience to his command, and had made the right assumption. That was why he was so furious.

Yes, she really *should* have pretended to be a tourist.

It was too late for that now, though. Too late to pretend anything, even that she wasn't the woman he'd spent the night in the forest with, not with this electricity crackling between them.

She really didn't want to obey him, since it felt as if she'd spent her entire life doing what people told her, but she was freezing, and if she stayed any longer in the water, she'd probably die of exposure.

Also, she'd never been good at pretending.

Gritting her teeth, Maude rose slowly from the water and he watched her, fury snapping in his dark eyes. She didn't look away, deciding she wasn't going to let him intimidate her, no matter that she hadn't told him about the baby. She had a stubborn streak in her, a streak her grandparents had tried first to whittle away and then to grind down, sanding off its sharp edges. Yet the moment Dominic Lancaster's dark eyes met hers, all those sharp edges snapped back into life as if they'd always been there.

She didn't bother to hide the rounded shape of her belly as she stepped from the pool and walked over to where her clothes lay, discarded on the grass. And she didn't speak as she picked up her T-shirt, fighting to stay calm as she dried herself off with it.

He merely stood there, his eyes dark, that muscle in his jaw leaping and leaping. It should have been threatening, the way he stared at her. Should have cowed her, made her feel ashamed of keeping the secret of their child from him, but strangely it had the opposite effect.

It put steel in her spine. If he was going to watch her dress, then he could watch. She wasn't going to hide herself or be ashamed. Because he was right, his hands had been all over her body, touching her hungrily and desperately. He'd wanted her and, from the growing flames in his eyes now, despite his fury, he wanted her still.

If he'd been the god of the forest that night, she'd been the goddess, and goddesses did not hide.

So she took her time, pulling her knickers up slowly,

then putting on her bra. Easing into her damp T-shirt then stepping into her jeans. He watched her the whole time, saying nothing, filling the air with a complicated mixture of hunger and fury.

She sensed somehow that he wasn't going to break the silence, that he wanted her to do it. Well, if so, too bad. If he could play silly games to keep her freezing in the water, then he could stand being the one to break the silence first.

Maude sat on the grass to put her shoes on—slowly— and only once she had did she get to her feet and stand facing him, meeting his hot black stare. She didn't speak. She only raised an eyebrow.

A thick, crackling silence filled the space between them.

'You're pregnant,' he said at last, and Maude experienced a brief thrill at making him break first.

'Gosh, really?' she said dryly. 'I had no idea.'

His jaw hardened still further. He took a couple of steps towards her then stopped. 'It's mine.'

Again, it wasn't a question, making his certainty needle at her. 'Is it?' She shrugged. 'Actually, it could be anyone's. There were a lot of men in the forest that night.'

Unexpectedly, he closed the distance between them and reached for her, gripping her upper arms, his fingers pressing hard against her skin, holding her fast. She tensed, staring challengingly up at him.

'It *is* mine,' he said in a low, hard voice. 'You did not sleep with anyone else. You were with me the whole night.'

A small thread of excitement wound through her, as if she liked his anger, liked the hard press of his fingers against her skin and the black flames that leapt in his eyes, the skein of darkness that wound through his voice.

That darkness that connected to something inside her the way it had that night.

It made her breathless, made her want to push him, make him savage as she had five months earlier. She had no idea why. Perhaps it was all about trying to re-create what she'd felt that night, as if she'd shaken off the rules society had imposed on her, free of everything but nature's own law.

'You don't know,' she said. 'I might have—'

'Don't lie to me,' he interrupted fiercely. 'Not about this.'

Get a grip. You can't lie about your own child.

Cold shock hit her as reality reasserted itself and she realised what she was doing. She'd enjoyed flexing her power over him, but she'd let it go to her head and that was a bad thing. That night with him, she'd let the fire inside her, the darkness, overcome her good sense and that was why she was in the situation she was in now. She needed to control herself.

Maude swallowed. 'Fine. Yes, I was the one in the forest that night and, yes, the baby is yours. I mean, probably.'

'What do you mean "probably"?'

He was very close, his hands burning her skin, the rich, spicy scent of him, the scent of the forest, all around her. He was tall, like one of the oaks towering over her, and very powerful, and she could feel the electricity of his presence, an elemental and raw thing that seemed to put its fingers around her throat and squeeze.

'Let me go,' she said, suddenly needing to put some space between them, because if she didn't get away from him, she wasn't sure what would happen. 'Let me go, *now.*'

Instantly, he released her, allowing her to take a couple of steps back. But fury in his eyes and the set of his powerful figure didn't change.

'Okay, okay.' She was breathing faster than she would have liked. 'Yes, the baby is yours.'

'You just said probably. Do you really want me to insist on a paternity test?'

She hadn't thought of herself as a proud person, but, as it turned out, she had a fair streak of pride in her too. 'No,' she snapped. 'It was you. I was a virgin that night.'

His dark gaze flickered. 'A virgin. That seems…apt. All things considered.'

She flushed, which annoyed her, and opened her mouth to make some retort, but he went on before she could get a word out. 'What the hell were you doing in the forest that night?' he demanded. 'The staff were warned to stay away.'

'I heard someone scream outside the cottage,' she said defensively. 'So I went out to check they were okay.'

'Screaming in the context of that particular party is nothing to worry about. Again, you were told—'

'I was worried,' she interrupted, defensiveness giving way to anger yet again. 'The forest isn't exactly safe at night and I wanted to make sure no one had fallen and broken their leg.'

'I see. And after that, you decided a little experiment with voyeurism was necessary?'

Again, she felt herself flush. Technically, he was correct, she'd been warned to stay away and she hadn't. Also, she realised belatedly that she hadn't thought about his perspective at all. He'd clearly thought she was a guest and had acted accordingly. He hadn't known she wasn't one, or that she was his employee. She'd been too caught up in the moment, in the magic of the forest and the night, and so had he.

That was why they were here, having this conversation, after all.

It's your fault and you know it.

Maude's jaw ached. She felt like she had at thirteen, when she'd had her one and only rebellion, and had sneaked out to a party given by one of the older kids at school. Her grandparents had somehow found out and her grandfather had come to get her, taking her by the scruff of the neck and marching her to the car. Then there had been an interrogation in his study the next day, with her grandmother standing beside his desk, arms folded. They'd had identical looks of disapproval and disappointment on their faces as they'd explained to her that she couldn't do the things that other children could. That she had her mother's wild blood in her and she had to be careful. She had to watch herself, had to learn to take responsibility for herself, had to learn self-control. They'd always made it clear that they were doing this for her own good, because they loved her, and so she'd tried. God knew how she'd tried, and mostly she'd succeeded.

But that night, none of the lessons had stuck.

And look what happened. Perhaps you're just like your mother after all.

Maude ignored the snide thought. 'I didn't know you'd run after me,' she said, knowing she sounded as if she was making excuses and, well… She was.

'Yes, you did,' he snapped. 'You wanted me to. You wanted me to catch you, too.'

'I was a virgin. Was I supposed to be carrying condoms, or—?'

'I thought you were a guest. All guests had personal responsibility for their own birth control. Condoms were also provided.'

'But not in the middle of the forest, clearly.'

He said nothing, dark eyes still burning with anger, the muscle in the side of his jaw flexing. The white stripe in his hair seemed brilliant in the sunlight, making the rest of the ink-black strands seem even darker, and she had the oddest thought that he looked like an angry badger.

'What are you smiling at?' he barked.

Maude hadn't realised she was, in fact, smiling, and stopped. 'Nothing.'

'I'm glad someone finds this situation so amusing.'

'It's not that. I just… Well, you looked… For a minute… Like…an angry badger.'

He blinked. 'A badger,' he repeated blankly.

'Yes. You know, with the stripe in your hair and—'

'I'm familiar with what badgers look like, thank you very much.' He tilted his head back slightly, looking down his aristocratic nose at her. The fury in his eyes had abated somewhat but the embers of it were burning still. 'And as much fun as this conversation is, I think we've come to the end of what we need to say to each other about that night.'

Relief washed through her. 'Oh, that's great. Okay, well, I'll just nip back to the—'

'You will come back to the manor with me, Miss...' He paused and frowned. 'What the hell is your name?'

She was very tempted not to give it to him, but that would be pointless considering he could find out very easily anyway. 'Maude,' she said. 'Maude Braithwaite.' She took a breath. 'And I'm sorry, but I'm not coming anywhere with you.'

Dominic couldn't remember ever being so furious. Furious enough that during the conversation with the nymph—*Maude*—he'd done a terrible job of keeping a grip on his temper.

That never happened to him. Normally he allowed himself to care just enough to be mildly peeved when things didn't go his way, but certainly not enough to provoke rage. Then again, 'normally' wasn't a word that could be attributed to his current situation, since there was nothing normal about it.

She was pregnant and the child was his, and *of course* the child was his. The fact that she'd even had a stab at pretending otherwise had incensed him, and he wasn't even sure why.

He wasn't sure how she managed to get under his skin so badly, but she did. There was something about the way she'd looked at him, all suspicion with an edge of wariness, and a slight hint of disdain that just…needled at him. Then that had faded to be replaced by anger, the gold in her eyes glittering bright, only for that then to vanish and be replaced by, of all things, amusement. Then anger again. So many emotional currents moving through her lovely eyes and flowing over her delicate features like a fast-moving stream.

If he hadn't been so furious himself he would have watched them move, captivated. But he was furious. Furious that she'd kept this pregnancy from him, and furious at himself that a) he hadn't used any kind of protection that night in the forest, and b) he'd suspected she wasn't a guest and he hadn't bothered to find out who exactly she was.

When problems occurred, Dominic dealt with them swiftly, since problems left unsolved usually compounded themselves, and so he was very aware that he had to deal with this particular problem just as swiftly.

He also didn't want to deal with it standing beside the waterfall, staring at Maude's T-shirt clinging damply to her body, making him remember how she'd looked standing naked in the water. She'd had a forget-me-not stuck to her skin just above one soft pink nipple and he couldn't get the sight of it out of his head.

With five months of celibacy weighing heavily on

him and his grip on his temper not what it should be, being here alone with her was a bad move and one he needed to rectify.

'Do you really want me to chase you again?' he asked, ruthlessly tempering his tone. 'Because we both know what happened the last time I did that.'

Her golden brows drew down and there was a long moment of silence. Then she said, 'Okay, fine.'

Part of him was disappointed at how easily she capitulated, his body wanting yet another chase, but he ignored that part of him. He wasn't going to make *that* mistake again, not considering the consequences of their last meeting.

Without another word, he turned and headed into the forest again, following the path back to the house.

Darkfell Manor had been built of grey stone in the late sixteenth century, and, in addition to the forest behind it, was surrounded by beautifully kept gardens, including a walled garden, a courtyard terrace, a formal parterre, a small orchard and a few fields.

Dominic had spent the majority of his early life here, and, after his father's death, he'd spent a not so small fortune ripping the interior out and getting a designer to redo the entire place.

Gone were the tiny, dark servants' quarters in the attic that his father had sometimes locked him into as a punishment. Gone were the hulking pieces of furniture that had crowded all the rooms, making him feel as if he were suffocating. Gone was the chill that had seemed to settle into his bones during winter because he'd failed in a negotiation with his father to keep the heating on.

Gone was the dark green wallpaper and the smell of old, damp stone, and the rooms that had felt as though they were echoing with the sound of his own loneliness.

Now, the manor's stately interior was all white, with polished floors and thick silken rugs, and light flooding through the tall, mullioned windows. It smelled of the beeswax that Mrs Harris used on the wood half-panelling and the lemon furniture polish she used on everything else. And it was warm, the interior redone with the best central heating system money could buy, that he could turn on whenever he wanted.

It was a jewel now, and, if Dominic was honest with himself, he almost regretted his decision to sell it. But only almost. This was the last remaining piece of his father's legacy and soon it would be gone, and good riddance to it.

After that, he'd finally be free.

He showed Maude into the formal sitting room with its view over the pretty parterre garden outside, sunlight flooding the windows and making the white walls glow. There was a deep window seat full of bright cushions, and a series of low white linen couches set in a box shape around the huge fireplace.

He gestured wordlessly to one of the couches and Maude sat on the edge of one of the cushions like a bird alighting on a windowsill, ready to take flight at any moment. There was a belligerent look in her eyes, which sent a strange thrill of anticipation through him, as if he was looking forward to whatever challenge she was going to throw in his way, and maybe he was.

The ennui he'd felt at the bacchanal had afterwards turned into an odd restlessness that he couldn't pinpoint or satisfy. It had been bothering him, and maybe, if not for the pregnancy, he might have turned all his attention on seducing this mysterious, oddly alluring woman, but...

Well. There was the pregnancy.

You're going to be a father.

The thought was cold and sharp, like a piece of thread edged with razor blades winding through his soul, cutting him in places he didn't expect. Places he'd thought were invulnerable.

He'd never wanted children. Never wanted to be a father, not after the hell his own father had made for him. He wouldn't have known how to be one even if he'd wanted to be anyway, yet it seemed now that he wasn't going to be given a choice.

Perhaps that was why he was so angry. He hadn't had a choice because she hadn't given him one.

It's not her fault. She wasn't expecting anything like that to happen that night, but you were.

The accuracy of the thought was so painful he ignored it.

'Why didn't you tell me about the baby?' he asked at last, after the silence had reached screaming point. 'No, scratch that. Were you *ever* going to tell me about the baby?'

A flush had crept into her cheeks, turning them deep

pink, making her brown eyes seem lighter. 'No,' she said without hesitation. 'I wasn't.'

That turned up the heat on his already simmering temper, but he kept a tight grip on it. 'Bold of you to assume I wouldn't want to know.'

'I read a few articles about you on the Internet, Mr Lancaster.' She was sitting straight-backed, with her hands resting on her thighs, fingers gripping her knees. 'And from what I read, you don't strike me as the family type.'

She wasn't wrong. He wasn't at all the family type. Yet the way she'd decided all of this, as if he had no say in how things were going to be, slid under his skin like a shard of glass.

She didn't know him and when she'd found out she was pregnant, she must have realised he was the father, and had clearly made some kind of judgement call based entirely on what the media wrote about him.

She hadn't bothered to speak to him personally, not once.

Why does it matter? When you never wanted kids in the first place? Throw some money at her and let her go on her way.

That was exactly what he should do. Yet he couldn't bring himself to do it. Something about the rounded curve of her stomach, the vulnerability of it, the knowledge that there was a little life curled there, a life he'd helped create, had hit him hard. Had woken something possessive and territorial in him that he hadn't known was there. He was never either possessive or territorial, since he didn't care about anything enough, but for this baby… Apparently he cared about that.

Maybe it was a primitive response to that night in the woods, with her virginity and how it had felt to be with her, sacred almost. Or maybe it was only biology kicking him in the teeth. Either way, he didn't like the intensity of the feeling or how it messed with his control.

'So what type am I, then?' he asked, still struggling to control his temper.

'Rich.' She said the word with distaste.

'You don't like rich people?'

'Not really.' Her stare was flat. 'I didn't like what I read about you either.'

'You assume the media always tells the truth?'

She frowned. 'There were lots of pictures of you at parties and—'

'You don't know anything about me, nymph,' he interrupted gently. 'Which means you have no idea what "type" I am.'

The belligerent expression on her face didn't change. 'So when was I supposed to "know" you?' she demanded. 'When you caught me in the forest after chasing me? Or maybe when you pulled me down on the bracken? Were we going to have a conversation about whether we wanted children or not then?'

His anger felt like a live wire, spitting sparks whenever he tried to grab hold of it, and he couldn't stop himself from saying, 'Perhaps if you'd bothered to tell me you weren't one of my guests, we wouldn't be in this position now.'

'Well, I didn't,' she snapped right back, her own temper clearly not within her control either. 'I was a little too busy being chased.'

Dominic opened his mouth to say something ill-advised, then thought better of it and closed it with a snap. This was getting them nowhere and being angry wasn't going to help matters. Because while he might not have chosen it, the child was his. He'd had a part in creating it, regardless of whose fault it was. The baby's presence was a fact, he couldn't change it, and being angry with himself that he'd been so careless, that he'd let his own desires take control, was pointless. He couldn't punish the child or Maude for his mistake.

His Greek mother had been one of his father's many lovers, and he himself the result of one night of passion and a careless attitude to contraception. She'd had him then had left him with his father, vanishing into the ether, never to be seen again. Jacob Lancaster had been very open with him, telling Dominic that he'd been going to put him up for adoption, but had then changed his mind. He'd needed an heir and now he had one.

Except Jacob hadn't been any kind of father to Dominic. He'd set himself up as a kind of business rival instead. Everything Dominic had wanted had had to be earned, had to be worked for or negotiated. Food. Clothes. Books. Toys.

Jacob had done this to teach him about the value of things and how to survive in the 'real world', where money was everything and the art of the deal the force that generated it. He'd wanted to turn his soft-hearted, sensitive son into an heir worthy of the great Lancaster Developments, with properties all over the world, that he had built up from nothing.

It had been a terrible childhood, but one thing Dominic would give Jacob: he'd become one hell of a businessman. But as to being himself a father, he had no idea how to do it, and he was too old now to learn, so claiming this baby as his was likely to be a mistake. He'd probably only end up repeating Jacob's mistakes. But…he couldn't walk away. Personal responsibility was something he believed in, and he was responsible for this.

'So, what were you going to do?' he asked at length. 'Bring the child up yourself?'

'Yes, actually.' She lifted her chin, stubborn as a mule. 'That's exactly what I was going to do.'

'I see. And you were going to bring up the child, in addition to your workload, here? Were you going to apply for leave to have the baby? You're only on a year's contract, remember, so you won't have much. What did you think would happen afterwards? And how were you going to manage childcare? Or did you think you could fob the baby off onto Polly while you worked?'

Instantly the golden sparks in her eyes ignited. 'I was not going to *fob* the baby off onto anyone! I'd only just started to think about—'

'Only just? What are you? Twelve weeks? Thirteen? More? You've known about it for a good—'

'There's a chance of miscarriage, you bloody idiot,' she retorted hotly. 'I didn't think there was much point—'

'Not much point?' he found himself interrupting yet again, his temper slowly slipping from his grip. 'A child isn't a damn puppy! You can't just give it back if you find you don't like it!'

'You think I don't know that?' She surged to her feet. 'If you've only brought me here to shout at me, then thank you but I think I've had enough.' She turned to the door and took a step towards it, but before she could take another, he reached out and grabbed her arm, holding it firmly, stopping her.

She rounded on him, her face pink, the gold flecks in her eyes molten with fury, turning the warm brown into bright guinea gold. 'How dare you?' she spat and tried to jerk away from him.

'Wait!' Dominic growled, holding on tighter. He didn't understand what was happening, how his usually expertly controlled temper had slipped so completely out of his grip. But no, of course he understood.

It was her and her temper. She was a flame and he dry tinder that kept igniting whenever she got too close.

She pulled her arm away but didn't keep walking. Instead, she faced him, her expression pure fury. 'Don't you manhandle me *ever* again,' she snapped furiously and then, much to his surprise, instead of leaving, she took a step closer. To him.

And Dominic found himself staring into her golden-brown eyes, watching the sparks of her fury turn into something else, feeling the air around them burst into flames with the same desire that had consumed them back in the forest that night. The same animal hunger.

He swore, then reached for her at the same time as she reached for him, and her mouth was on his before he'd even managed to close his arms around her. Hot and desperate, feverish, needy. As if she'd been as starved for him as he was for her.

He'd never experienced anything like it.

She bit his lip hard, pulling a growl from him, and then he was on one of the couches, and she was beneath him, and he was giving as good as he got, biting the softness of her full bottom lip, making her jerk beneath him as he devoured her.

She clawed at him, trying to pull aside his T-shirt as she squirmed and wriggled like an eel beneath him. He pushed his thigh between hers and leaned forward, pressing it against the sensitive place between her legs, making her gasp and writhe even more.

Then with quick, hard motions, he jerked her T-shirt up and over her head, then swiftly wrapped it around her wrists and pulled it tight, before pushing them up and over her head and down onto the cushions. Then he held them there.

She stared up at him, a golden-eyed fury, wildflowers still scattered through the heavy honey-gold skeins of her hair. The pulse at the base of her throat beat hard and fast and the heat between her thighs was insane, soaking through the denim of his jeans.

'You want this?' he demanded, his voice harsh gravel and rough sand.

She said nothing, but her eyes were full of anger and

heat, her hips moving sensually against the hard press of his thigh.

Dominic was a businessman through and through. His father had raised him to be ruthless, and ruthless he was. He had the soul of a predator and, right now, that predator was hungry.

'You have to tell me, nymph,' he said. 'And then you'll have to make it worth my while.'

CHAPTER FIVE

Maude lay on the couch beneath Dominic Lancaster's hard, hot body, a dim part of her screaming a warning. She couldn't quite work out how she'd got here, only that one moment they'd been shouting at each other, and she'd decided to leave, then the next she'd turned and thrown herself into his arms instead.

His mouth had been on hers and she'd still been furious.

Furious that he'd made her feel bad for how she'd acted. Furious that he'd made her feel afraid. Furious that, apparently, he wasn't going to laugh off her being pregnant with his child and let her resume life as if nothing had happened. Furious that he'd made her feel stupid for not considering her future, when a very deep part of her was still in shock that she was pregnant at all.

Furious that she wanted him so badly it was almost painful.

It was easier to kiss him than to talk to him. Easier to bite him and scratch him than it was to swallow her fury. Easier to channel that fury into desire than to keep hold of her temper and try not to lose it, not to be at the mercy of her wilder emotions the way her grandparents had always warned her about.

The way he touched her, with firm mastery, felt so good. Made her feel as if she could rage out of control, give into her darker impulses, and it would be fine, because he was there. He was strong and powerful and he could take anything she threw at him.

The way he'd bound her wrists made her feel contained and safe, which was weird since being tied up usually indicated the opposite.

He wouldn't hurt her, though, she knew that deep in her soul. He was the god of the forest and she was under his protection.

His dark brown eyes, so much darker than her own, bordering on black, stared down fiercely at her. Flames in them.

'Well?' he demanded, his rich, deep voice as dark as his eyes. 'What's it going to be?'

She took a gasping breath. 'Make it worth your while? What do you mean?'

'If it's sex you want, I'll give it to you. But then you will give me a calm, rational discussion about this baby.'

She did want sex. She wanted him to give it to her. But to talk about the baby…*their* baby…

'You can just walk away, you know,' she said thickly.

'I know. But sadly for you I'm not a man who walks away from his responsibilities.'

'You can walk away from this. I won't hold it against you.'

'No, but you'd rather other parts were against me,

wouldn't you?' He shifted his thigh between her legs, pressing delicately. 'Like this, hmm?'

Maude shuddered, the pressure causing the most exquisite pleasure. 'You don't want…children…'

'How do you know? I could want a whole horde of them.'

'But you…you don't.' A sound broke from her, torn from deep in her throat as he shifted again, the friction making her want to lift her hips against him.

He bent his head, his mouth close to her ear. 'Keep telling me what I don't want, nymph,' he purred. 'I'm sure you know better.'

This was insanity and she knew it. From the minute he'd shown up at the edge of the pool, watching her, she'd known it. Then being in this room, feeling as if the walls were closing in on her, because he was in it too, taking up all the space, all the air. Standing there like a king, with his arms folded, his black eyes accusing. As if she were one of his subjects and had to do what he said.

She didn't want to do what he said. She wanted to push him as much as he was pushing her, throw all her anger and frustration at him. She'd never felt so out of control and wild as when he was close, his electric presence making her feel as if she had a million ants under her skin.

It was ridiculous. As he'd so astutely pointed out, she didn't even know him.

Except…he made her feel *so* good. He made her feel alive and wild, the way the forest did, and she wasn't sure that was a good thing. But she couldn't think. He had his thigh right *there* and she was… God, it felt just right. It made her want to give him anything he wanted.

She struggled to take a breath. 'I…okay. A calm, r-rational discussion… That's…all?'

He shifted his thigh yet again and she writhed as sparks of pleasure shot along all her nerve endings. If this was what sex was like for everyone, then she couldn't think why anyone ever did anything else.

'You should have told me,' he said in that dark voice again, purring and soft. 'What kind of man do you think I am?'

His eyes were so dark, so deep she could fall right into them. Like Alice down the rabbit hole, she was falling and falling.

'I…don't know.' She was hardly aware of what she was saying, all her awareness concentrated on that delicious pressure between her thighs and the lines of his beautiful face. 'I looked on the Internet… Like I said… there were pictures…of you…'

'Not father material, hmm?' He moved and she gasped as a jolt of pure physical pleasure electrified her. 'Is that what you thought?'

She couldn't remember what she had thought. It was all becoming very hazy. 'I…just wanted to do it myself,' she said, her voice uneven. 'I…don't need you…t-telling me what to do.'

'Is that right?' For a moment he remained still, looking down at her, his dark eyes utterly impenetrable. Then abruptly he pushed himself away from her and off the couch, standing once again at his full height. 'In that case let's proceed straight to the discussion about the baby and you can give yourself an orgasm later.'

Maude blinked up at him, her arms still bound over her head, her legs lying open, the ache between them insistent. No. What was he doing? He couldn't just leave her like…this… Could he?

And apparently he could, because he didn't move, his arms folded across his broad chest, regarding her coolly, his expression giving nothing away.

A small pulse of fury hit her, that he could look so unbothered while she was lying here, desperate and hungry for him to finish what he'd started.

She swallowed and glanced down his body, looking for and finding evidence of his own arousal, pushing against the denim of his jeans.

He glanced down too, following the direction of her gaze, then shrugged, his mouth curving slightly. 'That's easily remedied. In the shower later.'

Bastard. He looked so unaffected while she felt… undone.

Did he want her to beg? Was that what he was doing? Or had he been offended when she'd said she didn't need him? Was he trying to prove a point?

In which case, he could go to hell. She *didn't* need him and maybe *she* was the one who needed to prove it.

Trying to get herself under control, Maude gave him her own version of his cool stare. 'Untie me, then. I'm not having a discussion with you like this.'

'Pity,' he murmured. 'You do make a pretty picture.'

But he reached forward and untied the T-shirt around her wrists. As the fabric fell away, Maude sat up, slightly startled to find him crouching in front of her, and before she could move, he took her wrists in his strong hands, chafing them gently.

His touch was warm and not at all sexual, and it took her by surprise. So much so that she just sat there as he glanced down at her wrists, presumably checking the blood flow.

Her grandparents weren't physically demonstrative. There were never hugs or affectionate touches, or kisses for her. There hadn't been comfort or reassurance. It was as if they didn't know how to express it. The most she'd ever had out of them had been the few times when she was sick or had a cold, and her grandmother would bring her a glass of water and some watery soup in bed.

So it was a little shocking to have Dominic Lancaster crouching before her, gently coaxing the feeling back into her fingers, his dark head bent, the stripe in his hair glaring white. There was a hint of grey at his temples too.

He was very close and he smelled so good, as he had the night they'd spent together. Of the spice of the forest and good, warm earth, and something else, something inherently masculine that made her mouth water.

'Why do you have a stripe in your hair?' she asked, the question popping into her head and then out of her mouth without any thought.

'I'm not sure,' he answered, as if he'd been asked the

same thing many times. 'I've always had it. My mother had the same.'

She stared at the stripe, itching to put out her hand and touch it. As if touching him was natural. As if he'd already allowed it. She stopped herself, though, her hands clenching into fists. No point in encouraging him.

He noticed of course and glanced up at her, his dark eyes enigmatic. 'If you want to touch me, nymph, you have to earn the right.'

Maude glared at him as he rose to his full height once again. 'I don't want to touch you.'

'Is that why you clenched your fists? Because you don't want to touch me?'

'The baby,' she said, deciding they had to get this conversation started so it could end and as soon as possible. 'That's what we were supposed to talk about.'

'Oh, yes,' he murmured. 'That's right. There's a baby. Almost forgot about that.'

'You were the one who—'

'I will not be cut out of my child's life,' he interrupted, his tone hard as iron. 'Do you understand me? I will be involved. You might not need me, Maude Braithwaite, but my child will.'

At the sound of her name, spoken in that voice, all darkness and heat, she felt another electric pulse. As if part of her had liked what he said and wanted it, which couldn't be true. She *didn't* want him involved. Her mother had brought Maude up on her own, without any help from Maude's father. In fact, her mother had never even told Maude *who* her father was, not that Maude cared.

Her grandparents had thought Sonya hadn't done a good job with her, but, despite that, her memories of the commune were good ones. She certainly hadn't suffered through lack of a father, and she'd make sure her own child wouldn't suffer either.

Except the look on Dominic Lancaster's face and the iron in his tone made it clear that he would brook no argument.

Her heart gave an odd little thump and, while she didn't want to admit it, a part of her was almost admiring of his willingness to step up and take responsibility for his child.

However, he also was who he was. A man with too much money, who apparently liked clubs and parties, all things that Maude didn't care about, and who almost certainly didn't value the things she did or wouldn't even be interested in them.

She didn't want him to be part of her child's life.

The child was *her* responsibility. She'd made a mistake, it was true, and she should have never done what she had in the forest that night. But now there would be a baby, and she couldn't shake off the feeling that somehow this child was a gift from the forest. It had been conceived in a way that still felt magical and sacred, even now. Perhaps if the man standing in front of her had been as deeply connected with nature as she was, then she would have felt differently. But he wasn't.

He was from the city and inhabited a different world.

The same kind of world that her grandparents inhabited, and she didn't want her child to have the same kind of upbringing she'd had. Where she'd been told what to do and how to be and how to behave. Been stuffed into the little box they'd prepared for her and never let out. Forced to grow into a shape that wasn't her own.

She wanted her child to be free to be their own person.

How do you know he doesn't feel the same way you do about it?

Well, here he was, already ordering her around and laying down rules, so of course he didn't feel the same way she did. That wasn't even a question.

'Why do you even want a child?' she asked belligerently.

'I didn't. But we can't always get what we want, can we?'

'Unfortunately,' Maude muttered. 'I can take the child away. You can't stop me.'

He lifted one dark brow. 'Do you really believe I can't stop you?'

Maude wished that she didn't, in fact, believe him, but there was a steely glint in his eyes that made her think that would be a mistake. He was a billionaire, with mountains of money and a whole bunch of lawyers on speed dial. Of course he could stop her.

He could take the child from you if he wanted to.

Something cold settled in the pit of her stomach. He had a hard edge, this man, a harder edge than she'd expected. He was rich and liked parties, but that didn't mean he was stupid. In fact, she had a feeling he was the opposite, and that while she had a stubborn streak a mile wide, he had a ruthless one as stark as the white stripe in his hair.

'Fine,' she bit out, trying to mask her trepidation. 'What kind of involvement are you talking about, then?'

'I want the child to live with me.' His eyes glittered. 'And that includes you as well.'

Maude's brown eyes widened and she blinked, her mouth opening slightly. Which satisfied Dominic far more than it should. About time he surprised her, because he was tired of her doing the same to him.

She wouldn't like what he suggested, he knew that already.

It was a tactic of his, to make outrageous demands and then see what the response was. Usually the response was a refusal, which was then his cue to start proper negotiations. From there, he would gradually give ground until it looked to the other party as if they'd got the best deal, when, in fact, they'd ended up giving him everything he wanted.

She would refuse, he knew, and sure enough, after a moment of shocked silence, she said, 'Are you kidding? I'm not living with you.'

There was no reason to feel a slight prick of irritation at that, yet he felt it all the same. 'It's not as if you'd be living on the street,' he said. 'I've got a substantial house in the middle of London and—'

'No,' she said before he could finish. 'I'm definitely *not* living in London.'

He wanted to argue, which was insane since the next step in his tactic was to concede minor ground until he got what he *actually* wanted. And surely what he actually wanted was *not* her living with him.

But then you'll have the child. And you'll have her in your bed. Why not?

He could think of several very good reasons why not. He'd only suggested it because it was the most outrageous demand, and one she'd never agree to. Yet now he'd demanded it, he couldn't stop thinking about it.

That moment on the sofa just before, with her writhing beneath him, obviously desperate for him, had been the most intense aphrodisiac he'd ever experienced, and it had taken almost everything he had to pull away.

But he'd never been intending to take it further. Again, she'd pricked his temper with her arguments and stubbornness, and he'd wanted to give her a taste of her own medicine, make her desperate, make her stop pushing him. Perhaps even make her beg for him.

Yet it had almost backfired on him. He'd become so distracted by the thought of her begging that his intention to stop had fallen by the wayside. At least until she'd insisted she didn't need him and…yes, again, he'd found that unreasonably annoying.

Everything about her was unreasonably annoying.

It had taken everything he had to pull away, but he'd managed it, and her look of surprise and irritation as he'd done so had made that worth it.

Except he was still hard and he ached, and he resented both of those things. That night in the forest he'd lost control and he'd found it freeing in the moment. But that moment was gone and he didn't want to want it again. He didn't want to want *her*. Every interaction with her felt fraught, as if he were walking a tightrope between his control and her undeniable physical pull, and even the slightest wrong move would cause him to lose his balance and fall.

He'd never experienced a feeling like it and he hated it.

He hated, too, that the thought of her living with him, or, more accurately, her being in his bed, was far too tempting to ignore. He'd been so restless lately, not wanting any woman in particular, and it wasn't until that moment on the couch that he'd realised that he did, in fact, want a particular woman: Maude.

'What's wrong with London?' he asked, trying to cover his irritation.

'I don't like the city,' she said. 'I never have. And I don't want to bring my baby—'

'*Our* baby.'

'*The* baby up in a city.' She was glaring at him again. 'He or she is connected to the forest and needs to grow up as part of the natural world.'

The muscles in Dominic's neck and shoulders were getting tense. He uncrossed his arms and thrust his hands into the pockets of his jeans instead. 'The baby can visit the natural world in London,' he said tersely. 'There's parks and woods, all sorts of natural phenomena.'

'It's in the city,' she said insistently. 'Those parks and woods are surrounded by houses and roads and train tracks and streets. We created the baby here and he or she needs to live here.'

Dominic stared at her, utterly bemused. Her hair was drying into a wild tangle of curls and waves, and the bedraggled remains of wildflowers were still caught in amongst the golden strands. The gold in her eyes was glittering, her delicate features flushed with temper, and she looked very much like a wild creature he'd somehow caught. There was something wild about her, too, something untamed, that made him want to catch her, tame her to his hand…

Maybe his demand that she live with him wasn't so outrageous after all. Maybe that was what he *did* want, so he could have that magical experience of that night in the forest again. And again and again…

'Well, he or she can't live here,' he said. 'Because I'm selling the manor and the forest along with it.'

'What?' She paled. 'But you can't do that.'

This time her obvious shock didn't give him any satisfaction, because if he wasn't much mistaken that was a glint of pain in her eyes. As if he'd taken something precious from her and ground it into the dust.

'Why not?' he asked, feeling vaguely as if he'd made a mistake and resenting that too. 'It's my manor and my forest. I can do what I bloody well like with it.'

'But…' She stopped and her mouth compressed into a hard line, her chin jutting mutinously. 'Who are you selling it to?'

'I don't know yet.'

'I'll buy it.'

He nearly laughed. 'Oh? You have a few million pounds lying around, do you?'

She flushed. 'No, but I'll… I'll save up. My grand-parents were going to gift me some land further north that I was going to use to rewild. But I can sell that.' She shoved herself off the couch after a moment, standing in front of him, all righteous indignation. 'I'll go to the bank and borrow as much as I can. I'll do unpaid work. I'll sign a contract—'

'Why?' he asked, cutting off the flood of words, mys-tified by her sudden passion. 'Why on earth do you care so much about Darkfell?'

She was silent, biting her lip. Then she said simply, 'I love the forest here. It feels like…like…home. Like… I belong here. The baby was conceived in the forest and so the forest is connected to it. I know that sounds strange and I don't expect you to understand, but that connection to nature is important. I feel very strongly that this child needs to be born here and that he or she needs to grow up here.'

She was right, he didn't understand. That she, who had no connections to this place, should feel so passion-ately about it, while he, who'd actually grown up here…

For years he'd put Darkfell to the back of his mind, visiting it only in midsummer, for the bacchanal. He never thought about it when he wasn't here—it was very much a case of out of sight, out of mind. But it had always felt like a millstone around his neck, dragging him down.

It wasn't so much the place itself, though that was part of it.

It was what it represented.

His father, Jacob Lancaster. Who'd made him beg for everything he'd needed. Or rather, not so much beg—the distinction was important—but explain why he'd needed it. List the pros and cons, present a case for payment, 'sell the idea', as Jacob had put it. Dominic had had no money with which to pay for it, and so everything he'd made a case for had had to be put on his 'tab', a growing debt that he could never pay off.

When he was thirteen, his father had presented him with a full accounting of that debt, expenses incurred throughout his childhood, including food, clothing, schooling and the wages of a nanny when he was very young.

To Dominic back then the debt had seemed astronomical. He'd had no hope of paying it back, or so he'd told his father, weeping. But Jacob hadn't cared. It was a lesson in how to do business and was it unfair? Yes. But life was unfair. Life was also open to negotiation, so state your case, negotiate the costs, cut them down, change my mind and on and on. Stop crying. Harden up. Figure out the deal.

So Dominic had. He'd hardened up, had figured out the deal, and had cut the costs of his upbringing in half by the time he was fifteen.

At seventeen, when his father had died of a heart attack, Dominic hadn't expected to inherit Lancaster Developments. He'd been sure his father had put one last obstacle in his way and, indeed, Jacob had. The will had specified that, since Dominic still owed him for his upkeep and hadn't proven himself adequately, the company would instead go to Jacob's second in command.

But Dominic had been waiting for this moment, planning, and doing deals just as his father had taught him. He'd used those lessons to wrestle the company back under his control and then, once he'd had it, he'd broken it up into tiny little pieces and sold every last one.

Now, he owed his father *nothing*.

Darkfell was the last of it.

'How strongly?' he asked, his brain turning over.

'What do you mean?'

'I mean, what would you do to stop me from selling it?' He arched a brow. 'What would you give me?'

She looked puzzled. 'Are you asking about money? Because I don't have—'

'It's not money I'm talking about.'

'But... I don't have anything else.'

With another woman he might have suggested sex, since it was clear that she wanted him every bit as badly as he wanted her. But she wasn't another woman and he didn't play such games with innocents like her. She was far too sincere, too honest, and, apart from anything else, he'd lost control of himself so completely the last time they'd had sex, he had no desire to do it again. Especially given the severity of the consequences the last time it had happened.

That didn't mean she had nothing to give him though.

'Yes, you do.' He allowed his gaze to settle on her stomach, where their child rested. 'You have plenty to give me, nymph.'

Instantly fire leapt in her eyes, and she put a hand protectively over her little bump. 'You'd really use our child as a bargaining chip?'

Both the gesture and the sharply worded question sent an unexpected arrow of discomfort through him, and he found himself brought up short by a sudden realisation.

This game they were playing together, he'd just fallen into it. The game of negotiation and bargaining, of making a deal, was as natural to him as breathing. He did it all the time, in his work and when he was with a woman, bartering and negotiating for money or pleasure, it was all the same to him.

But this, with a child in the mix and a woman who didn't play games…

You can't do that with her. It's wrong and, worse, it's no better than what your father did with you.

The arrow of discomfort turned cold and sharp.

How lowering. To be like his father in any way, shape or form. Especially when he'd always seen himself as the very opposite.

'Of course not,' he said coldly, drawing himself up. 'I would never use the child. The bargaining chip is Darkfell, the manor and the forest. If you don't want me to sell it, then I'll hold off until the child is born. You can also continue to live in the groundskeeper's cottage. But in return you will make no argument about any obstetric care I see fit to employ or any discussions about custody arrangements once the child is born.'

Her eyes narrowed, her hand still curled protectively over her bump, which angered him for reasons he couldn't articulate. Did she really think he was dangerous? That he would hurt her or their child? He would never do that. *Never.*

'I want paid maternity leave for when I have the baby,' she said flatly.

Normally he would have loved that she'd joined in his negotiation, giving him demands of her own, but there was something about the way she still had her hand over her stomach, protecting their child from him, that incensed him and, worse, made him feel ashamed of himself.

'Naturally.' He tightened his grip on his temper that kept on lunging like a rabid dog on a short leash. 'I'm not a monster. The child is mine, after all.'

She studied him for a moment, chewing her bottom lip, and he didn't like that at all. He had his armour, the facade of the jaded, bored playboy that he'd been wearing so long it had become part of him. But now she was looking at him as if that armour wasn't there at all, as if she could see through him, all the way to the small, angry, hurt boy he'd once been.

'Well?' he demanded, the word sharp as a pistol shot.

'So, what?' She was seemingly oblivious to his mood. 'You'll sell Darkfell after the birth?'

Dominic snarled inside his head and choked the life

out of his temper. Give nothing away, that was key to this, the key to any good deal. Maintain a good poker face.

He shrugged. 'Perhaps. And perhaps not.'

It was only marginally satisfying to see how that needled her and it must have, because she scowled abruptly. 'What does that mean?'

'It means that, unfortunately for you, I'm the owner and I get to say whether I sell it or not.'

'Why do you want to sell it?'

'None of your business.' His temper was still there, snarling behind the bars of the cage he'd set around it, which meant that probably the best thing for him to do right now was to leave. 'Well?' he asked, with the merest hint of his usual insouciance. 'Do we have a deal?'

She wrinkled her nose. 'I suppose so,' she said at last.

Normally he would have reached out and shaken her hand, sealing the deal between them and leaving her with a sensual reminder of his touch. But her hand was still guarding her stomach and her gaze was wary, and for some reason that was food for an anger that had no reason for being and no outlet, and he was tired of it. Tired of her getting under his skin. Tired of being here in this house and her hand over her stomach as if he was a threat.

So he didn't shake her hand.

He only gave her a sharp nod, then turned on his heel and walked out.

CHAPTER SIX

A WEEK LATER Maude sat at the kitchen table in the manor, glowering at her laptop screen and all the emails she hadn't responded to. It was the Your Girl Friday team all wanting to know what was happening with her and why she hadn't been sending anything to the group chat.

It made her feel tired.

She really should let the others know that she was okay and that everything was fine, and she *should* tell them that she was pregnant, but she couldn't face it. Not when all she could think about was Dominic Lancaster storming out of the manor sitting room in a huff the week before.

And yes, he *had* been in a huff.

She wasn't sure what she'd done to annoy him so much, but it had been something. He'd been all barely repressed heat right up until the moment he'd started bargaining with her about the manor and then, quite abruptly, he'd gone cold. At least his voice had been cold. His dark eyes, on the other hand, had been full of banked embers, as if she'd offended him in some way.

Perhaps he wasn't used to people talking back to him. Then again, John and Polly had never had a bad word to say about him, and they were pretty free with their opinions if they didn't like something.

He'd certainly been angry when she'd told him not to use their child as a bargaining chip. In fact, that was when his voice had turned to ice, so in retrospect, yes, she *had* offended him.

Maude bit her lip, annoyed with herself. Why was she thinking about him? She had a million tasks to do today and not one of them included thinking about Dominic Lancaster. Yet she hadn't been able to get him out of her head. The bold white stripe of his hair. The touch of his fingers as he'd gently chafed her wrists. The heat in his eyes as he'd bargained with her, only for that to disappear in a flash of temper as she'd put her hand on her stomach protectively.

He really hadn't liked her accusation or her being protective of the baby, and she suspected he hadn't liked that because… Well, the only logical assumption was that she'd offended him by assuming their child needed protection from him.

Maude leaned on her elbow, hand tucked beneath her chin as she stared sightlessly out of the large kitchen windows and into the walled garden beyond.

He had *not* appreciated her assumption that he was a threat, and she supposed she could understand that. In her defence, though, she didn't know him and their little confrontation in the sitting room had been one shock after another. All she'd been able to think about was protecting her child—that had been instinct. She didn't believe he'd *actually* hurt her or anything else, yet...

The god of the forest will claim his due.

The thought whispered through her head, sending little prickles of heat flooding over her skin. His hard thigh between her legs, pressing insistently against her...

Her mouth dried and she swallowed.

No, she couldn't allow thoughts like that. And she especially couldn't allow him to see his effect on her, to think he got under her skin, because she had a feeling that if she allowed him any quarter, he'd take all of it. He'd take everything and she had little enough as it was.

All this week she'd been uneasy, waiting for him to text or to call or email or contact her in some fashion, to talk about these 'custody arrangements' he'd mentioned the week before, yet she'd heard nothing.

A doctor had turned up a couple of days after Dominic had left and had given her a thorough examination, which she'd allowed since that was what she'd promised. The doctor had also asked if she wanted to know the gender of her child and she'd automatically said yes without really thinking about it.

A boy, apparently. She was going to have a son.

Dominic should know, of course, but she'd decided to wait until he came back to Darkfell so she could tell him face to face, and instructed the doctor accordingly.

But the uneasy feeling wouldn't leave her, and she wasn't sure why. She couldn't settle to any task, not fully, and even walking in the forest, which usually

soothed her, hadn't helped. She felt like Damocles waiting for the sword to fall.

Abruptly, she pushed the laptop shut and leaned back
in the chair, folding her arms.

She needed to make a decision. She needed to figure out just what she wanted when it came to the baby
and his demands to be part of the child's life, because
when he did come back, he'd no doubt try to steam-
roll her into doing whatever he wanted, and that wasn't
going to happen.

She'd had years of being told what to do, of having
to bend herself into the shape other people expected of
her, and she wasn't going to start doing it again for him.

So. The first thing she was going to insist on was that
the child be brought up here, at Darkfell. The forest was
where he had been conceived and that and the manor
were part of their legacy, and Dominic Lancaster would
sell it over her dead body.

She was responsible for, not only the child, but the
forest as well and she'd protect them both, no matter
what he wanted. Of course, if that was her position,
then she was going to need to think of how she could
get him to agree.

She needed some kind of leverage, something that he
wanted that she could use to extract a promise from him
that he wouldn't sell Darkfell. And why did he want to
sell it anyway? The manor was lovely, and the gardens
around it were amazing. How could anyone get rid of it?

She glanced around the kitchen, which had been ren-
ovated very recently and very sensitively, she thought.

There was lots of light and big windows. White cabinetry and polished wooden floors. A lovely, airy space.

Him wanting to sell, not only the house, but the forest too, mystified her. She'd asked him why, but he hadn't been in any mood to tell her, that had been clear. Was it money? Had he made bad investments somewhere? Then again, the articles she'd read about him all pointed to him being exceptionally good with money, so maybe not that. But what other reason could it be?

Not that she was interested. That was a side issue. All she needed was his agreement not to sell it, and in order to get that, she needed to find out what he wanted. Except the only thing she could think of was the baby, and she couldn't—wouldn't—use her child in that way.

Perhaps she could guilt him into it by pointing out that Darkfell was his child's legacy, and getting rid of it was wrong. Surely, he couldn't argue with that. But… what if he did? What other things could she use?

Maude continued to stare fiercely out of the window as her thoughts spun.

What could she use to nudge him in the right direction? What did she have that he wanted, apart from the child?

You know damn well what he wants.

Her breath caught. Lying under him on the couch, her wrists tied with her own T-shirt, his dark eyes full of hunger as he looked down at her…

Her. He wanted her.

Heat returned, prickling over her skin once more as

her thoughts spun a little faster, and this time she didn't force herself to stop thinking about it.

Could she use their chemistry to get him to keep Darkfell? Use his physical response to her in some way? Perhaps seduce him into keeping Darkfell? It was certainly worth considering. He had all the power here, that was the problem. He was her boss and a well-known, infamous billionaire playboy, while she was just a contract worker. Still, she wasn't without weapons. She wouldn't use the baby, but she could certainly use her femininity.

She'd never thought of her sexuality in that way before, mainly because she hadn't cared about her sexuality before. It had felt like one of those traps her grandparents had warned her about that could lead her down the wrong path if she gave into it. At that stage, she'd still been trying to be what they wanted, so she'd been a good girl and had concentrated on her schoolwork instead of boys. Then, when she'd gone to university and met the other Your Girl Friday women, the vagaries of sex and dating had felt too complicated. Sex had just seemed to make people unhappy and, anyway, she'd much rather be out in the woods than in some bar trying to pick up some guy.

But things were different now. He'd made them different. He'd woken something in her, something dark and hungry, and the thought of using that hunger to make him do whatever she wanted held a certain…appeal.

Careful. It might backfire on you.

Yes, that was a risk. She wanted him, too, and the

tricky part was that, while she was fairly confident she could seduce him, she had no experience of staying in control herself.

And she had to stay in control. That was the only way with a man like him. He'd bound her hands that moment in the sitting room, and she'd felt strangely safe rather than afraid, but she didn't want that to happen again. Didn't want her own hunger to take the reins. She couldn't cede him any control, because once she did that, well…

You'd be powerless again.

A memory returned, of her standing by her grandparents' car where she'd been told to wait while they talked to her mother. Of her not knowing what was going on and trying to ignore the growing suspicion in her gut that, whatever it was, it wasn't going to be good. No one had told her what was happening. All she'd been told was that her grandparents were taking her out for an ice cream, and she was to go with them and not cause a commotion.

She'd stood by the car and watched as her mother had glanced once at her, shrugged, then walked away.

That had been the last time she'd seen Sonya.

Her grandparents had bought her the promised ice cream but then they'd told her that she would be living with them from now on. Then she'd been thrust into a new living arrangement, in an unfamiliar environment, with people she'd barely known. She'd cried, of course, heartbroken at being taken away from the commune and her mother. Her grandparents had ignored her the way they always did when she 'made a fuss'. She'd never felt so powerless and she was not going to let that happen again.

Just then, Polly came bustling into the kitchen, breaking the train of Maude's thoughts.

'Well, Mr Lancaster is on his way,' Polly said as she began opening cupboards and putting things away. 'He'll be staying a couple of nights.'

Maude was conscious of a little shock arrowing down her spine. 'H-he is?'

'Yes, just got a text from him.' Polly straightened and gave her a concerned look. She was a motherly woman and Maude liked her quite a bit. 'You're looking a bit peaky, love. Are you quite all right?'

The Harrises didn't know about her pregnancy. No one knew except the doctor and Dominic Lancaster, and Maude didn't particularly want to tell Polly now. Not when there were so many things undecided.

'I'm a bit tired.' She pushed the chair back and stood, picking up her laptop. 'I might go and have a lie-down.' She paused a moment. 'He won't want to see me, will he?'

Polly shook her head. 'Oh, no, I shouldn't think so. Not sure why he's here. Probably something to do with the sale.'

Maude stilled. 'You know he's planning on selling?'

'Oh, yes. He's been talking with John and me about it for a couple of months. A good thing if the manor goes to someone who will actually live here.' Polly pulled open the dishwasher and began unloading it. 'The house needs a family and Mr Lancaster isn't about to start one any time soon.'

Maude found her hand was creeping to her stomach again. 'You don't think he will?'

'No, love,' Polly said, her attention on the dishwasher. 'He's not a family man.'

She should go, let Polly continue cleaning up, but she didn't move. 'Do you…know him well?'

If Polly found her curiosity startling, she didn't show it. 'Known him going on about ten years now,' she said, methodically unloading some teacups. 'When John and I took over management here. This was his childhood home, apparently, but he never visits. He only comes for his midsummer parties and that's it.'

Maude's curiosity deepened. She hadn't known he'd grown up here at Darkfell. Interesting. And perhaps another thing she could use to get him to keep the place.

'Do you know why he's selling it?' she asked.

Polly shut the dishwasher. 'No and it's not my business either. John and I are due for retirement, so I won't be sorry. It's a big place to look after with just us.'

As if on cue, the rhythmic thump of helicopter rotors came drifting through the air, and Maude was conscious of a sudden electric thrill pulsing through her.

'Oh, that's him,' Polly said. 'Better get on with airing out the bedroom.' And she vanished out of the kitchen door.

Maude took a breath as the sound of the helicopter came closer and closer.

He was coming and he would want to talk to her, in

which case she'd need to prepare herself, as well as decide what demands she was going to make. Because there *would* be some demands.

She just hoped he'd be prepared for them.

As his helicopter settled on the grassy lawn at the front of Darkfell Manor, Dominic stared grimly out of the window and wondered for the millionth time just what the hell he was doing.

He didn't need to visit his childhood home physically. He could have rung Maude and talked to her or sent her an email or even a text. Except he hadn't. He'd organised his helicopter and here he was, and he still didn't understand why.

He'd spent the past week keeping busy with client meetings and investigating a couple of new investment opportunities—something he normally loved doing. He'd also thrown himself into attending multiple parties, including the opening of an exclusive new club in London. There had been the usual celebrities, socialites, a few royals and captains of industry all in attendance. Again, usually something he enjoyed.

Yet as he'd sat in the VIP area with more than a few beautiful women all vying for his attention, he'd felt… dissatisfied. And, worse, bored. The same boredom that had been dogging him for months, along with the same restlessness. It was infuriating.

He'd wanted to enjoy himself with a few casual liaisons, yet every time he even looked at a woman, all he could see was the challenging glint in Maude Braithwaite's brown eyes and the way her hand had curved over her stomach. All he could think about was the feel of her in the forest that night, and how then she'd looked up at him when she'd been beneath him on the couch, her face flushed with heat and passion...

None of the other women he'd met had that same glint in their eyes, and while they definitely looked at him with heat and passion, it didn't move him. It didn't make him hard.

His nymph had put a spell on him and now she was all he thought about.

Ringing her to discuss the baby hadn't even occurred to him. Neither had simply sending her an email or a text. All he'd thought was that any discussion with her had to be conducted face to face, so he'd let Polly know he'd be visiting, and now he was here, he wondered if he'd made the right choice.

Then he wondered why the hell he was doubting himself, when he never had before.

It was her that was the issue. It was all her and the baby.

He'd thought about the baby, too, in the past week. About how he was going to be a father and what that would look like. Not like his own father, that was for sure. He wouldn't keep his child secreted away like an afterthought. He wouldn't go away and leave them for weeks and months, rattling around in this big ancient house. And he certainly wouldn't be presenting them with itemised bills for their own upkeep or making them negotiate for everything they wanted.

The child would live with him in London and he'd give he or she whatever they wanted, whenever they wanted it. And as for Maude, well, she could come and live with them too. He hadn't had a mother, since his own had up and vanished, and he'd never known why she'd just walked away—his father had never mentioned it and Dominic had never asked—but maybe his life would have been less lonely, less difficult, if she'd stayed. He certainly wanted his own child to have their mother around.

One thing for certain, though: neither of them would live here.

The helicopter settled and Dominic leapt out, heading for the path that led to the groundskeeper's cottage rather than the manor, since he might as well get this meeting with Maude over and done with, and as soon as possible.

The cottage was a ridiculously picturesque brick building on the edge of the forest, not far from the manor house. It was small, with a slate roof and ivy climbing up the sides and pots of lavender just outside the front door.

He hadn't been here for years, he realised suddenly as he approached the cottage. Not since he was a boy. Craddock, who'd been his father's gamekeeper, had lived in it, and Dominic had loved visiting him, though Jacob had disapproved. He hadn't liked his son mixing with the staff.

Jacob would have a fit now, Dominic reflected as he knocked on the door, if he'd known that his son was now having a baby with said staff.

There was a pause, and he was about to knock again, when the door opened and Maude stood on the threshold, her warm brown eyes meeting his.

And he felt it again, that gut punch of desire, leaving him breathless, his heart racing in a way it hadn't raced for any of the women he'd surrounded himself with back in London.

His fingers itched to shove the door open, grab her and pull her close, press his mouth to hers and taste her again. But he crushed the urge. This was not about sex. This was about the child.

'May I come in?' he asked, when she didn't say anything.

'You didn't tell me you were coming,' she said, eyeing him.

'No,' he agreed. 'I didn't. Do you really want to have this discussion on the doorstep?'

She stared at him a moment longer, then turned without a word, and went down the little hallway. He stepped inside, closing the door behind him, then followed her through another doorway and into the tiny living area.

It was a cosy little room, with a sofa facing the fireplace and an armchair to the side. There were throws of various brightly coloured fabric draped everywhere and lots of mugs on the small coffee table in front of the sofa. Books were stacked in piles on every available surface, as well as magazines open at the crossword section. A comfortable room, full of cheerful clutter, that made him feel at ease, though he wasn't sure why.

Maude stood in front of the fireplace, her arms folded,

regarding him warily. Her hair was loose and she was wearing a flowing, wraparound dress of deep scarlet that shouldn't have been so sexy, since it was very plain. Yet somehow it drew his attention to every one of her feminine curves, including the generous swell of her breasts and her little bump, making him feel once again that primal sense of possession.

Yours. She is yours.

He gritted his teeth, ignoring the thought. The baby was his. *She* wasn't.

'Why didn't you warn me that you were coming?' she said, as if *he* were the problem.

He sat on the arm of the sofa, ostensibly casual, trying to find his usual lazy, bored facade. 'Should I have?'

'I would have appreciated some preparation.'

'Preparation for what?'

She opened her mouth as if to speak, then, clearly thinking better of it, she shut it. But he didn't miss the way her gaze darted down over his chest and lower, before returning once again to his face. Colour bloomed in her cheeks and the little glints of gold in her eyes gleamed brighter, and the rush of possessiveness and desire tightened its grip on him.

She wanted him too, that was obvious.

'So,' she said after a long moment of silence. 'Are we going to have a discussion about the baby? Since I assume that's why you're here.'

Straight to business, was it? Probably a good thing, considering the attraction that he'd hoped would have eased in the week he'd been away apparently hadn't eased at all.

It irritated him, dug beneath his facade, made him want things he shouldn't and now he was starting to regret coming here. Why had he thought face to face was better? This could have been a phone call.

'There will be no discussion,' he said flatly. 'I have made my decision. The child will come to live with me in London.'

Hot temper leapt in her gaze. 'Absolutely not. You will not be taking my baby away from me.'

'I'm not going to be taking the baby away from you,' he said. 'You'll be coming too, naturally.'

Her arms dropped and she took a step towards him, every line of her radiating anger. 'No,' she snapped. 'I'm not going anywhere. The baby should be brought up here, in Darkfell, close to the forest, not in a city. Not in London.'

'As I said, this is not a discussion.' He tried to keep his tone mild and his expression bored. 'My son or daughter will be with me and since I will not be living here, neither will they.'

'Why do you think living in London is better than living here?'

'Why do you think living here is better than London?'

A moment of silence fell, tension seething in the room. She was breathing fast and he found his gaze drawn to the deep V of her neckline and the shadowed valley between her breasts. It wouldn't take much to get her naked. Just a tug on the tie holding her dress together and it would fall open…

Get your head out of the gutter.

Dominic gritted his teeth. 'You promised me you wouldn't argue. I distinctly remember that.'

Her chin jutted. 'That was when you said this would be a discussion and not just you telling me what to do.'

Taking a slow, even breath, Dominic gripped hard onto his temper. It was ludicrous that she should have such an effect on him and ludicrous that he should let her. He'd had decades of perfecting his control and he wasn't going to let one young woman get under his skin so easily no matter how lovely she was.

'Well, you can't stay here, nymph,' he said at length. 'I will be selling the manor once the baby's born, as I've already mentioned.'

Her eyes glittered with heat. 'Polly said this was your childhood home.'

'Yes,' he bit out, even more annoyed now. Polly should never have said anything. 'It is.'

'Then why do you want to sell it? Don't you want to pass it on to your child?'

'No.' The word was far more emphatic than he'd meant it to be. 'My child will have nothing to do with this place.'

'Why not? It's their legacy.'

Why was she asking so many questions? He didn't want to talk about Darkfell, especially not with the mouthful of angry, bitter words that had somehow gathered in response. In fact, it was surprising just how bitter and angry they were, considering all the time that had passed. His father shouldn't still have such a hold on him, not after so many years.

'It's not a legacy I would wish to pass on,' he said after a moment, choosing his words carefully.

She frowned, as if she found his response puzzling. 'Why not?'

He forced himself to smile. 'Let's just say my childhood here wasn't a happy one and leave it at that.'

She studied him for a long moment, the temper dying slowly in her eyes. 'I…feel the same way about the city if you must know,' she said, a little hesitatingly. 'My mother used to live in a commune in Scotland, but my grandparents didn't approve of me being brought up there so they came and took me away to live with them.'

He could have sworn he wasn't curious about her, not in the slightest, and yet now he found himself studying her in much the same way as she'd studied him, as if she were something new and interesting he'd never seen before. Strange when there was nothing new and interesting about people in his experience. They all wanted the same things, which pretty much boiled down to money, power, or sex. He didn't care to know about their motivation for pursuing one or all of those things, not unless it applied to a deal he was doing, so it was quite astonishing to find himself almost intrigued by what she'd said.

Clearly being taken away to live with her grandparents hadn't been a good experience. Was that why she was resisting him taking their child to live in London with him?

'I only want happiness for our child,' he said slowly. 'I don't want to take them away from you. A child needs a mother.'

Something shifted in her eyes, though he couldn't have said what. 'But I don't want to leave here,' she said. 'And I don't want to live in the city.'

Frustration coiled inside him, but he crushed it. 'Oh? Why not?'

'I love being part of nature. It's important. The trees and the forests, all the wild places, are important. They're part of me. And I feel responsible for them. I want to protect them, and I want my child to learn how to protect them too.' As she spoke, her eyes glowed, the warm brown like a sun-dappled forest pool, glinting with gold and amber.

She meant every word, he could see that. There was a passion and a sincerity in the words and in her expression too, that tugged at something inside him, something he couldn't quite articulate.

There was no sincerity in his world, no honesty. It was all games and power-plays, all deals and money, smoke and mirrors. And as for passion, well, there was none of that either. Passion was a weakness, a vulnerability for someone to exploit for their own gain.

Looking at Maude now, all Dominic could think of was that she shouldn't tell him these things, shouldn't show him such a vulnerability, because—and he knew himself far too well—he'd use that passion and sincerity against her. Use them to get what he wanted, because what he wanted, he got. He didn't know why he cared, but he did.

'You shouldn't tell me these things, nymph,' he murmured softly. 'You shouldn't reveal your hand before you've sealed the deal.'

Her eyes narrowed. 'Why not?'

'Because now I know what cards you're holding, I can use that against you. For example, you want me to keep Darkfell? Very well, I will. On condition that you and the child come and live with me in London.'

CHAPTER SEVEN

THE LIVING ROOM of the cottage felt too small, too claustrophobic. Maude felt as if she couldn't get enough air. Dominic Lancaster was standing in the middle of the room, filling the entire space with the taut electricity of his presence, and it was hard for her to think.

She'd thought she'd been prepared for him, but of course she wasn't.

She'd hurried into the cottage as his helicopter had come in to land, racing into her bedroom to pull out one of the few dresses she owned that she could still wear, a red one Irinka had once told her had looked beautiful on her.

Certainly, when she'd pulled open the door to his knock and his gaze had dropped to the neckline of the dress, she'd felt a small burst of satisfaction. That was until she'd taken him in and realised that no amount of preparing herself for meeting him was going to be enough.

He was in a suit today, perfectly tailored to his tall, powerful figure. It was of dark grey, with a black business shirt, and with a silk tie of washed gold. Beautiful clothes for the most beautiful man.

And he was beautiful. Not a god of the forest today, but a god of industry, or business. Zeus presiding on Olympus, using the power of his charisma and authority to dominate the other gods.

Her heart had begun to beat fast, and she'd forgotten everything she'd meant to do, all the demands she'd meant to make. She'd intended to take control of the conversation, but he'd taken it instead, laying out his demands and leaving her to protest in a pathetic knee-jerk reaction.

It made her feel childish to have to say no like that, but what else could she do? She'd told him why she wanted to stay here, had let some of her passion for the forest show in her voice and she'd thought that might sway him.

But it hadn't, she could see it in his eyes.

He'd been right to warn her. She'd let slip too much and he was far too astute a businessman not to use that against her. Her plans for seducing him into not selling the house and leaving their baby with her probably wouldn't work either, not when she didn't have the experience to play that game.

There is another option: refuse to play.

The thought whispered in her head, appealing to the broad streak of stubborn inside her. He was bending her to his will with all this talk of deals, trying to make her use his language, operate by his rules. And she'd fallen into it without thinking.

But she wasn't a dealmaker and she didn't negotiate. She was a free spirit and he couldn't force her to be what he wanted her to be. She had to be herself.

Maude took a breath. 'No,' she said.

'No?' One winged black brow rose. 'What do you mean no?'

'I mean, I'm not coming to live with you anywhere.'

His dark eyes glittered. 'Then I will sell Darkfell.'

'Fine. Sell it.' She lifted her chin, her heart beating suddenly far too fast. 'I'll continue to live in the cottage.'

'I have money, nymph. More money and power than you can imagine. You think I won't use them to—'

'Do it,' she interrupted, digging down into that stubborn streak of hers. 'Get your lawyers. Sell this house. Have the police come to the door and try to arrest the woman pregnant with your child.'

The lines of his face had hardened, the air in the sitting room full of his thick, crackling anger. He looked like Zeus ready to pick up his thunderbolt and hurl it straight at her.

It was exhilarating to affect him this way, to make his bored, jaded mask slip a little.

'I'm not playing your game,' she said into the seething, tense silence. 'I won't. I've done what other people wanted me to do all my life and I'm not doing it now. This is too important.'

'Important to whom?' There was a certain lethal softness in his voice. 'Is this little performance really for your child's benefit or for your own?'

That caught at her in a place she wasn't expecting, a

vulnerable place, making a thread of doubt wind through her. This was supposed to be about her child and yet…

You were brought up in Earthsong by your mother, because she wanted to stay. It wasn't about what was best for you, was it?

Selfish, that was what her grandparents had always said about her mother. Selfish of Sonya to bring Maude up in a place where there was no formal schooling and no other children, either. Living in the commune had been lonely, and Sonya had left a large portion of Maude's care with other people, if any were around. Most of the time she'd been left on her own.

Was she the one being selfish now? With her own child? Forcing her or him into a way of life that they might not necessarily want or might not be the best for them?

Maude turned around abruptly, facing the fireplace, not wanting her doubt to show, and especially not since he'd already warned her once about that.

She didn't want to be a mother like her own, who'd cared more about herself and what she wanted than she had about what was right for Maude. So…maybe her child would be better off in London. Dominic could certainly give him or her a much better life than Maude could give them on her own. And living in London didn't mean they had to be apart from nature. There were plenty of woods and lakes and wild places that were within easy reach of London, as he'd already said.

Abruptly, the familiar, intoxicating scent of the forest surrounded her and she knew he was there. She could sense him standing behind her and close. Like one of those mighty oaks in the forest, tall and strong. And she had the oddest urge to lean back into him and take some of his strength for herself, because she was coming to the end of hers and pure stubbornness wasn't a good enough reason to keep fighting him.

'Maude,' he said quietly. 'Tell me why this is so important to you.'

Dominic had made an error somewhere along the line and he knew it. He'd known it the moment she'd turned away suddenly, his little barb about her passionate outburst obviously landing somewhere painful.

He hadn't known what hurting her would do to him, because if he'd known, he wouldn't have done it. He hadn't expected to feel as if he'd kicked something small and vulnerable, and purely for cruelty's sake.

He couldn't believe he'd done the same thing as he had last week, letting himself be drawn into a fruitless argument because she was so stubborn, and then nearly losing his temper because she wouldn't give in and because no one said no to him.

The problem was, she'd called his bluff. She'd absolutely refused to negotiate, leaving him no choice but to bring out the threat of lawyers, knowing, even as he'd said it, that he wasn't going to do that. He wasn't going to tear the child away from her or trespass her from Darkfell.

He wanted to sell this place, that was true, get rid of the last vestiges of his father, but it surely didn't matter when he sold it. It wasn't as if he needed the money. He was insisting purely because she aggravated him so much.

He was letting his emotions get the better of him.

He wasn't in the habit of caring about other people's feelings, so it was odd to care about hers. Or at least to have her hurt bother him as much as it did. Perhaps it was because of that passion, that sincerity. The honesty burning in her eyes as she'd told him that nature, the forest, was important to her.

It was foreign to him, that honesty, that sincerity. In the past, in the boardroom, they had been ammunition in the negotiating war, and he'd used both to win. But he wasn't in a boardroom now, and she wasn't a businessperson who knew the rules of engagement.

She was pregnant and it wasn't a deal they were negotiating, but what would happen when their child was born. She was right, this was important, and they needed to find an understanding between them, not relentless arguing.

So his request to know why she was so insistent about staying here had been a start of the bridge they had to build between them, a small olive branch to begin with. Also, he was curious.

She didn't move and he realised he was closer to her than he should be. Enough to be aware of the scent of lavender that seemed to come from her hair and another delicate, very feminine scent that was uniquely her own.

It made his mouth water, woke everything male in him into a state of almost painful alertness.

'I grew up close to nature,' she said, without turning around. 'I spent a lot of time in the commune's gardens and in the woods nearby. It was a…child's paradise. The commune didn't have a school or lessons of any kind, so I was free to follow my own interests. Then my grandparents took me away to live with them. And there were schools and lessons and timetables and…rules. I tried to live with them, tried to fit in, but it never felt the same as being in the commune. It never felt like…home. Not the way the forest does.'

Finally, she turned around and looked up at him, her brown eyes dark, the forest pool shadowed. 'I wanted that for our child. I wanted him or her to experience the same freedom I had at Earthsong, to not be bound by rules and timetables, even if it's only for a short time.' Slowly the gold in her eyes began brightening. 'It's important for our future society that we come to an understanding with nature, with this planet we live on. Because this is our home, and we need to take care of it.'

Dominic found himself momentarily transfixed, caught by the passion in her voice and the glitter of it in her eyes. And he realised, almost with shock, that although she'd revealed a significant vulnerability to him, he wasn't going to exploit it for his own gain, use it against her to get what he wanted.

And not only he wouldn't—he *couldn't*.

She believed what she said, believed in it totally, and her refusal to play the little game he'd started made him feel something akin to shame for his own part in it. She had more integrity than he did, it seemed, and part of him admired her for it.

'Then,' he said quietly, 'you should stay here.'

She blinked, as if she didn't quite understand what he'd said. 'You mean stay here? In the cottage?'

'Yes.'

'But what about selling Darkfell? I thought you were adamant the child has to live with you.'

'I'll hold off selling the house for now.' He was still standing far too close to her, and it was all he could do to keep his gaze on her face and not the neckline of her dress. 'All of this is a moot point until the child is born anyway. We can decide what the future will look like then.'

Shock rippled over her features and he couldn't deny that pleased him. 'I don't understand. What changed your mind?'

'You did,' he said simply.

'But I didn't offer you anything.'

'You did, though. You offered me your honesty and your sincerity, and I found that a…compelling argument.'

Her forehead creased. 'Why?'

'Because honesty is a scarce commodity in my world. So is sincerity. It's refreshing.'

She studied him for a long moment, the currents of her emotions shifting and changing in her eyes. 'It wasn't honesty that I was going to offer you,' she said at last.

A soft husk now threaded through her voice, making everything in him go very still. 'Oh?' he murmured. 'And what was it that you were going to offer me?'

Colour flushed her cheeks. 'You changed your mind without it, so I don't need to offer it now.'

A sharp electric jolt went through him, as if he were a hunter and had suddenly caught the scent of prey. Surely she could not be saying what he thought she was saying? 'Now who's playing games?' he said softly. 'Tell me.'

Her mouth curved in a smile that maddened him, as if she knew a secret that he didn't, which was impossible. Because if, as he suspected, she'd been intending to offer him her body, then there was nothing he didn't know. He'd been playing the game of sex and seduction for decades now and he knew everything there was to know about it. Certainly more than this little nymph did.

'If I tell you, that'll leave me with nothing to use against you later.' Her gaze dropped to his mouth and then back up again. 'I need to have something in reserve.'

Her skin was warm, her scent utterly intoxicating. There was something about it that seemed to grab him by the throat and not let go.

'If it is what I think it is, then you're not the only one with a weapon,' he murmured, lowering his head until his mouth was bare inches from hers. 'You have to be careful, nymph. If you play with fire, you might get yourself burned.'

Her eyes, so close to his, darkened and, as he watched, the lush softness of her mouth opened slightly.

'I don't mind,' she whispered. 'Especially if you burned with me.'

Again, there was that honesty, reaching inside him as much as her scent did. Though it didn't grip him by the throat so much as it wrapped long fingers around his heart. And he didn't know why.

Another woman would have kept playing with him and he would have enjoyed it. He would have won in the end, of course, because he always did, taking things to their logical conclusion, which would be in the bedroom.

But Maude wasn't playing now. She'd given up the game, even though she'd barely started, and now had handed the win to him. Yet he couldn't shake the feeling that he hadn't won at all, that she had.

Heat glittered in her eyes, and hunger. For him. She didn't look away and she didn't try to hide it. She wanted him and he felt a strange sort of protectiveness well up inside him in response.

'You shouldn't look at me like that,' he said. 'You shouldn't show any kind of vulnerability to a man like me.'

'Why not?'

'I already told you. I'm a businessman and I'll exploit any weakness I find if it serves my interests and gets me what I want.'

'Would you though? Would you really?'

It was a genuine question. He could see it in her eyes. 'You put your hand over your stomach last week,' he couldn't help but point out. 'And you told me not to use our child as a bargaining chip. So you tell me. Would I?'

She studied him for a long time, desire bright in her gaze and yet also, shining through that, a sharply acute intelligence that made something in his heart skip a beat.

You want her to say, No, you wouldn't.

He wasn't sure what that thought had to do with anything. Because he knew the truth, which was yes, of course he would. He'd exploit any weakness, because, like it or not, that was the lesson he'd learned from his father. That was how he'd survived.

And it still hadn't been good enough for him.

The thought was snide, stealing through his brain, but he shoved it aside. Then he let go of her and stepped back, because maybe, after all, he didn't want to know what kind of man she thought he was.

'Don't answer that,' he said smoothly. 'And I should leave. You're a pretty thing, but I've already had everything you have to offer. I don't need to revisit it.'

It was a cruel thing to say, but he had to put some distance between them. She also needed to know that he wouldn't allow anyone to have power over him that he didn't grant them. And the only thing he'd granted her was that she could stay here. He hadn't given anything up.

He thought she would back away, thought that she would be hurt, and he'd intended both. Except she didn't back away and it wasn't hurt that glittered in her eyes, but anger.

'Is that right?' She reached down to the tie of her

dress and casually pulled it. 'I suppose you won't care about a reminder, then.'

The fabric fell slowly open, revealing the fact that she was wearing nothing underneath it. Not a stitch. Only warm golden skin, pink nipples and the sweetest thatch of golden curls between her thighs. Only the swell of her stomach where their baby lay.

Your baby.

She lifted her chin and stared straight at him, openly challenging. And Dominic found that he'd been right, she *had* won this little game they were playing, and that he didn't know quite as much about sex and seduction as he'd thought he did.

Because right now, he couldn't move. He couldn't breathe. Desire and hunger had tightened their grip around his throat and were slowly, relentlessly squeezing. The raw possessiveness of that night in the forest was welling up inside him, an animal feeling, turning him into nothing but instinct.

He knew he should turn around and walk away, prove to her once and for all that she had no power over him, and especially not sexual power. *He* was the master of that, not her, and yet…

She let the dress fall slowly off her shoulders and flutter to the ground, and then she closed the distance he'd put between them, not once taking her gaze from his. As bold as she had been that night in the woods, only this time it was bright daylight and he could see her. He could see every bloody inch.

Christ. He wanted her.

She halted in front of him, and laid one small hand on his chest. 'I think you're a liar, Dominic Lancaster,' she murmured. 'I think revisiting it is exactly what you want to do.'

CHAPTER EIGHT

MAUDE WASN'T QUITE sure what she was doing. Somehow the conversation had got away from her and somehow her control had got away from her, too. Somehow he'd taken it and he'd done it simply by existing. By being close. By telling her she could stay at Darkfell, that he wouldn't sell it after all, and without demanding anything in return.

Her honesty, that was what she'd given him apparently, and that was what he'd been happy with, or so he'd said.

Except she didn't believe him. He'd told her that he was a businessman and that he exploited every weakness, and yet he hadn't exploited hers. He could have used her love of the forest against her to get her to do anything he wanted, but he hadn't.

She knew what he wanted though, and a part of her wanted him to admit it. To test whether she actually had the power she thought she did, power over him. He'd tried to distance her with words, but he hadn't meant them, she knew that. Not when she could see the blatant heat in his eyes.

It was bold of her to strip naked before him, but it wasn't anything she hadn't done before. He'd seen her by the pool and, in the forest that night, he'd run his hands over every inch of her. So she felt no embarrassment or shame, even though perhaps she should have felt both.

She only wanted to see if she was as powerful as she felt in this moment. Prove to herself, and maybe to him too, that the power she remembered from that night in the forest was still hers. The power of a primal goddess.

She needed it. Needed to know once and for all that she could unsettle him as badly as he unsettled her.

Desire flared in his dark gaze now, like embers of a banked fire igniting into life, and it made her heart race. The heat of his body burned through the cotton of his shirt and into her fingertips where they rested on his chest. He smelled so good, like all the wild places deep in the forest, where she could lose herself if she wanted…

'You shouldn't do this,' he said softly.

'Why not?' She lifted her other hand and placed that on his chest too, testing the hard muscle she could feel beneath his clothes. 'It's nothing we haven't done before.'

'Sex will…complicate matters.'

'Really? I thought you were an infamous playboy.' She stepped even closer, the tips of her breasts grazing the cotton of his shirt. 'You're not supposed to care about sex complicating things.'

The fire in his eyes leapt higher and yet still he didn't move. 'Consider the last time we did this.'

'I am considering it.' She ran her fingertips down the front of his shirt, to the waistband of his trousers. 'What's the problem? It's not as if I'm going to get pregnant again.'

The breath hissed in his throat as her fingertips dipped lower, over the hard length of him she could feel through the wool of his trousers.

'I have never been a possessive man.' His dark voice had roughened. 'But I should warn you that I'm feeling very possessive now. I'm not sure you would appreciate me wanting to own you.'

He was doing it again, trying to put distance between them. Trying to frighten her, she thought. Sadly for him, she wasn't easily frightened.

She looked up into his eyes as she let her fingers trace the outline of his hard shaft, watching the flames in his eyes leap even higher. 'I think you're afraid,' she murmured. 'Is it me you're afraid of?'

He bared his teeth. 'I didn't say you could touch me, nymph.'

It wasn't exactly an admission, but he'd betrayed himself all the same. He *was* afraid, though what of she didn't know. Because as she'd already told him, he was an infamous playboy and sex was the one thing he shouldn't be afraid of.

Maude dropped her hands and stepped back. 'That's fine. I don't have to touch you.' She turned. 'I'll get my—'

But she didn't have a chance to finish. His fingers closed hard around her upper arms and he pulled her around to face him. 'I didn't say leave,' he growled, then his mouth was on hers in a kiss so hot and hungry, she almost lost her mind.

Then again, perhaps she'd lost it already, because the moment his lips met hers, she was up on her toes, sliding her arms around his neck, pressing her body against his as she opened her mouth to him, letting him take anything and everything he wanted.

Heat exploded between them, a conflagration burning high.

His hands came down on her hips, gripping her, turning her so that the couch was nearby and then he took her down onto it, crushing her beneath him. He was a solid, hot wall of muscle and there were too many clothes between them. She clawed at his shirt, ripping it open, and he cursed, grabbing her hands and holding them away from him.

'No,' he said roughly, black eyes molten. 'If you want this, then I'm in charge.'

She sucked in a breath, her heartbeat wild, her body trembling with need. It hadn't been like this between them in the woods that night. No one had been in charge then, they'd both taken what they'd wanted and it had been so good. But then that night they hadn't known each other, hadn't known what would happen and nothing had existed then but the moment.

They couldn't have that moment again. It was gone. And her god of the forest was now hidden behind the mask of Dominic Lancaster. A mask he seemed very set on keeping.

She wanted to ignore him, keep tearing at his clothes until she'd uncovered the man he was behind the mask, all raw heat and primal power, nothing but glorious essence, but there was iron in his black eyes. He wasn't going to yield. If she wanted this, she was going to have to surrender to him.

It wasn't a choice. She wanted him and if this was the only way he could give himself to her, then she'd take it.

So she nodded, the resistance bleeding out of her.

He shifted, rising up to his knees. With calm, deliberate movements, his black gaze not leaving hers, he undid his tie, pulled it off then leaned forward, looping it around her wrists and pulling it tight. Then he lifted her hands and took them up and over her head, pressing them back down onto the couch cushions.

She took a gasping breath as she lay there, looking up into black eyes full of flames. He stretched himself over her, his big, long body all muscled power and heat, and, really, she should have been frightened by how helpless she was. He could hurt her, he could do anything he wanted with her, and she could do nothing to stop him.

Except she wasn't afraid and she didn't feel helpless. He wanted her, his desire bright in his eyes, and that was where her power lay. In surrendering to him, in giving him her trust.

A strange thing to think about a man she didn't really know. Then again, it wasn't Dominic Lancaster she was surrendering to, but the man he was beneath that. The man she'd met in the forest that night.

That man hadn't hurt her, hadn't done anything she

hadn't wanted. That man had given her everything she'd demanded and then had demanded the same of her. There had been nothing between them that night, nothing held back, nothing hidden. Trust given and pleasure received.

He still hadn't moved, searching her face. 'What are you thinking about? Are you afraid?'

'No,' she said truthfully.

'Why not? Some women would be.'

'They might, but…I trust you.'

His body tensed, something moving in his eyes, gone too fast for her to read. 'And why would you do that?'

'That night in the forest. We were strangers and yet there was trust between us. And you gave me no reason to regret it.'

His black gaze was pinned to hers. 'But we're not in the forest now.'

'I know, but I think you're still the same man.' She shifted beneath him, watching the flames in his eyes leap again. 'You don't need to hide him. Not from me.'

He stared at her silently, his gaze boring into hers and he didn't move. Not even when she lifted her bound hands and looped them around his neck. Not even when she pulled him down and kissed his beautiful mouth, giving him everything the way she had that night, holding nothing back.

Perhaps it was then that the mask of Dominic Lancaster slipped, because he made a sound deep in his throat, and abruptly his tongue was in her mouth, exploring, tasting, devouring, his hand between her thighs, stroking, exploring.

She gasped as his fingers slid over her slick flesh, teasing her as his mouth ravaged hers. There was no finesse to it, no art, but she didn't care. They hadn't had any the last time in the forest and they didn't have it now. But she didn't need it. She needed only him.

He paused long enough to open his trousers and then he was down on her again, holding her hips down on the couch cushions as he pushed into her in one deep, hard surge.

She groaned, wrapping her legs around his waist, her hands gripping hard to his shoulders, nails digging into the fabric of the jacket he still wore. He slid a hand beneath her rear, tilting her, sliding deeper and she made another sound, pleasure spreading through her like a wild, dark fire.

He didn't speak and neither did she. It was as if they couldn't talk again until this chemistry or need or whatever it was had burned itself out. She could only gasp as he rocked deeper and harder, her legs tight around him as the pleasure climbed higher and higher.

He kissed her neck and she felt the sharp edge of his teeth against her skin. It made her shudder. Made her remember that night again, and how they'd connected. At a base level, at essence, the both of them animals in the dark, their civilised skins left far behind.

She wanted that again so she turned her head to find his mouth, kissing back hungrily and hard, and then he was moving faster, and the pleasure was tightening, the net it had caught her in constricting around her. She didn't want it to end so soon, and yet she wasn't going to be able to last, she knew it.

His hand was down between them again, giving her that last bit of friction, and then the ecstasy caught her, dark and hot, and relentless as the tide.

Maude cried out as it hit, shaking and shaking, feeling his movements get wilder and almost out of rhythm until he lowered his head and buried his face in her neck, a groan of release escaping him, too.

Dominic lay there, knowing he was likely crushing her, yet utterly unable to move. It had been a long time since an orgasm had stunned him like that, if one ever had. But no, that night in the forest he'd been stunned, he remembered. Apparently being stunned was a theme with Maude.

Aftershocks of pleasure pulsed through him, the sweet, musky scent of sex and her filling his senses.

He hadn't meant to break like that so completely and maybe he should have been worried about how easily he had, but with the most blissful post-orgasmic sense of satiation filling him, he honestly couldn't bring himself to care.

He'd thought binding her hands would give him some control over the chemistry that had burned white-hot between them, at least until she'd told him that she trusted him. And then proved it.

It had been a gift, that trust. It had reminded him of that night with her, where they hadn't needed anything but each other. No rules, no barriers, and no reason not to give each other everything.

There had been such simplicity in that, and he'd realised as he'd looked down into her eyes that he wanted that simplicity again.

And she'd given it to him with no deals, no quid pro quo. She'd offered him pleasure, given him all her passion, holding nothing back, and, yes, it had been simple.

But he could feel the hard swell of her stomach between them, where his child lay, and that made this whole situation anything but simple.

He shifted off her, gathering her in close so that they were lying on the couch with her half on him, and then glanced down at the rounded curve of her belly. She said nothing, her eyes still half closed.

Feeling oddly hesitant, he reached down to trace that curve, touch where his child lay. It was a strange feeling to know that between them they'd created this little life, who now lay still, waiting to be born. Then, as he was wondering that, another feeling swept over him, the knowledge, sure and deep, that he would do anything to protect that little life. Anything at all, even give up his own.

He'd always been a selfish man. His father had taught him that selfishness was the only way to get ahead, and that was a quality Dominic had had to cultivate if he'd wanted to be the heir Jacob had wanted him to be.

It had never been something he'd questioned… Until now.

His child was more important, he understood. More

important than anything else in the entire world, and certainly more important than he was.

Did your father ever feel this way about you?

The thought crept through his head before he could stop it. And of course, he already knew the answer. No, Jacob hadn't felt that way about Dominic. Because if he had, he'd never have made Dominic's life such a misery.

Maude shifted and put her hand over his, moving it slightly, and to his utter amazement he felt something flutter against his palm. He looked at her in shock. 'Is that…?'

Her lovely mouth curved in the most beautiful smile he'd ever seen. 'Yes. I felt him kick for the first time a couple of days ago.'

Instantly Dominic sat up, cold all over. 'I was lying on you. I could have hurt—'

'No,' Maude interrupted. 'You didn't hurt him.'

'Him,' Dominic heard himself repeat stupidly.

She nodded. 'I had a scan last week. I wanted to know the gender. I…was going to ask you if you wanted to know, but…'

He. Dominic was going to have a son.

Yet another feeling washed over him, colder this time and full of doubt. This baby was getting more real by the moment and he hadn't once thought about what kind of father he'd be. The baby had been only a thought, an abstract, but now…

It hit him then, like a thunderbolt straight from heaven, the certainty that he would *never* be the kind of father his own had been. His son would not be left alone, his son would not be handed an itemised account of the cost of his upbringing. Like Jacob, Dominic had never wanted children, but unlike Jacob, he would embrace being a father. He would give his child everything he'd never had growing up, attention, protection, tenderness and care.

This would be the purpose of his life now, because this was the thing he'd been looking for, the next challenge to throw himself into, and he would not fail. He couldn't.

'I'm sorry,' Maude said.

Dominic looked at her, for a second not processing what she'd said, his head too full of the epiphany he'd just had. 'For what?'

'For not telling you that we were having a boy.'

He blinked, her face suddenly leaping into focus. Delicate features, tawny gold brows, warm honey-golden skin, dark gold hair in soft waves around her face. His nymph.

Your child. Your woman.

The power of the thunderbolt was resonating inside him, spreading out from the baby, spreading wider, becoming possessive and intense. Part of him wanted to deny it, because he never felt that strongly about anything and never wanted to, except it was there in his heart, as relentless and inevitable as the tide.

This woman and the child she carried were his now, and it was time for him to claim both of them.

Maude was looking at him with some concern. 'Are

you okay?' she asked, sitting up slowly, her hair falling around her shoulders.

She was astonishingly lovely, naked like this, with the beautiful swell of her stomach beneath her full breasts, and his breath caught.

She was why he'd been so restless and tense. *She* was why he didn't want any other woman. Which made *her* the answer to the problem.

If he wanted any peace at all, he needed to be sleeping with her. No longer resisting her, but indulging himself fully and to the utmost, and with no one else but her.

It felt foreign to think that, to limit himself that way, yet, instead of feeling constrained, he suddenly felt as if he'd been given a freedom of sorts. As if it had been the resistance that had constrained him rather than the other way around.

'I'm fine.' His voice sounded rough even to his own ears. 'But I have decided something.'

Her gaze flickered and he could see the apprehension in it. She thought he was going to demand again her presence in London, that was obvious. Well, she was wrong. He'd already made that demand and she'd protested, digging in when he'd threatened, and he didn't want to make that mistake again.

Demanding things from her didn't feel right, not after what she'd given him just now on the couch, the gift of her trust. And it was a gift. She'd given him the same that night in the woods back then, but he hadn't realised its value until now. And now he knew…well. He wasn't going to throw that away.

'I understand why you don't want to come to London,' he said. 'In which case, I'll come here.'

Her eyes widened. 'What?'

'I'm tired of London. I'd rather be here where I can keep an eye on the baby, and where I can have you.'

A flush crept through her cheeks. 'Have me?'

He held her gaze steadily. 'I've been thinking about you for months, nymph. Thinking about that night. I tried to put it out of my head when I woke up and found you gone, because I thought I wouldn't see you again. Then there you were, swimming in the forest pool, and I knew it was you instantly.' He paused, letting her see that he was telling the truth. 'I haven't had a woman since you and I find I don't want one. The only woman I want at the moment is you.'

A shocked expression rippled over her face. 'But… why?'

'I don't know,' he admitted. 'You're unlike any woman I've ever met, and perhaps it's only physical chemistry, but… What I do know is that it's been impossible for me to think of anyone else.'

Her lashes lowered abruptly, veiling her gaze, but she didn't move. 'So…what are you thinking?'

'No, don't do that,' he ordered softly. 'Look at me.'

Her lashes lifted and she met his gaze, apprehension in it.

'You don't want me here?' he asked bluntly. 'Because if so, that might be too bad since I own this house and the grounds.'

'It's not that.' Her chin firmed in that stubborn way he

was beginning to recognise. 'I'm not your girlfriend or your wife, and I don't want to be either of those things. And I won't be your...' she made a gesture with her hand '...brood mare that services you whenever you're in the mood, either.'

Strangely, now he'd made a decision, the restless tension that had been gripping him receded. Perhaps it was merely the aftermath of his rather stupendous orgasm, but he felt lazy and sated, and the sight of her pretty golden eyes sparking with temper amused him rather than annoyed him.

'A brood mare,' he said slowly as if tasting the words. 'Yes, you'd look very pretty with a halter on, in a stall. Though I think you'd bite so maybe you should have a muzzle.'

She scowled. 'I wasn't joking.'

He let his amusement go. 'I know. So how about this? I will live in the manor and you live in the cottage. We will have our own lives. But at night...I could sleep with you or you could sleep with me, I don't mind which.'

She sniffed. 'You're assuming I'm going to want to sleep with you.'

Dominic moved his hand slowly, giving her plenty of time to pull away, sliding his palm beneath one round breast and cupping it gently. 'You don't want to sleep with me?' he asked casually, stroking his thumb back and forth over her nipple in a lazy movement. 'Because of course, if you don't want to, I won't make you.'

She swallowed, her eyelashes falling again, a soft breath escaping her. 'I... I...might not want you.'

'You might not?' Very gently he pinched the tip of her nipple, making her gasp and shudder. 'You'd better be clear about this. I wouldn't want to make any mistakes.'

She'd begun to press herself into his palm, arching her back slightly. 'I mean…there might be times when… I don't want you at all…'

'Of course,' he murmured. 'In which case I'll respect your wishes. But you're a passionate creature and I think those times will be few and far between.' He bent and gently circled her nipple with his tongue, before drawing back and blowing gently on it, making her shiver all over. 'Don't you?'

She gave him a frustrated look from underneath her lashes. 'You're manipulating me.'

'Yes,' he said, unrepentant because he was getting hard again and all he could think about was being inside her. 'But all you need to do is say no and I'll stop.' He took his hand away. 'Shall I stop?'

Her chin jutted as she glowered at him. 'Did I say stop?'

She looked adorable just then, pink with arousal, golden eyes glittering with desire and frustration, and he couldn't help but take her hand and guide it down to the front of his trousers. 'Just remember that manipulation can go both ways,' he murmured. 'And what works on you, also works on me.'

Her expression changed, becoming thoughtful, and he couldn't stop the heated rush of anticipation that flooded through him in response.

You want her to have that power over you?

Not exactly. But he wasn't averse to it either. She had no guile, this woman. She wasn't going to use it against him, not the way he would. And it was odd to think that even as she'd given him her trust, he was giving her his.

'Try it,' he invited. 'Try it on me and see what happens.'

She didn't need to be asked twice and soon proved his point, much to their mutual satisfaction.

CHAPTER NINE

MAUDE CHECKED HER WATCH. It was nearly twelve-thirty, the time Dominic had told her to meet him by the waterfall. Apparently, he had a 'surprise' for her and she'd been thinking about it all day, conscious of a building anticipation that felt a lot like excitement.

She'd been experiencing that more and more often in the past week, since Dominic had relocated himself to Darkfell Manor.

When he'd first suggested living at Darkfell, she'd been instantly wary. She hadn't been sure why he'd wanted to be here for a start, and then she'd wondered if it was so he could be a control freak about the baby. Certainly, after the day they'd ended up having sex on the couch in the cottage, and he'd felt the baby kick, he'd suddenly started deciding things and expecting her to go along with them.

He was a man who liked to take charge of a situation, and yes, she'd been wary about what would happen when he arrived here. Not that she'd had a choice in the matter. He did own the place after all.

She'd thought the instant he'd moved back, he'd be

at her door, demanding sex, since that seemed to be the implication after he'd seduced her again on the couch. Yet…he hadn't.

In fact, the day he'd moved in, he'd stayed in the manor all day and she hadn't seen him at all. She hadn't seen him the next day, either. The third day had come around with still no sign of him, and she'd felt…disappointed. And she'd hated that she'd felt disappointed, because what did it matter if he clearly wasn't as desperate for her as he'd led her to believe? It *didn't* matter. Not to her. She'd gone without sex long enough that another couple of days weren't going to make a difference.

It wasn't until the third night that he'd appeared on her doorstep. She'd opened the door to find him lounging against the doorframe, and all he'd done was raise an enquiring brow. That had been enough to find herself in his arms, her mouth on his, hungrily devouring him as he'd devoured her.

They'd spent the night together every night since then, and usually they didn't talk. They gave in to their own mutual hunger and let that guide them instead, and in the morning she always woke up to find herself alone.

That was good. That was what she preferred. Living her life bound by nobody's rules but her own.

Except she found herself looking forward to the evenings when he'd visit more and more. And sometimes, when they were in each other's arms, she'd catch herself wondering what he was thinking. Wondering why he wanted to sell Darkfell. Why his childhood hadn't been a happy one and why he didn't want to talk about it.

Maybe it was a good thing to be curious about him, though. She was having his child after all, and she should know more about him than that he was a billionaire with a hugely successful investment firm, who was also very good in bed.

She didn't know what this promised 'surprise' was, since this was the first time he'd wanted to see her during the day, but she could feel the familiar breathless excitement that she felt every night the moment she heard his knock on the cottage door.

Did he want to repeat their night in the forest, but during the day? Was that what the surprise was? If so, she wasn't averse to it, not at all.

She walked along the little path that led to the grassy clearing with its waterfall and pool, the trees eventually giving way and opening out ahead of her.

Dominic was already there, sitting on a blanket that had been laid out on the grass. Also on the blanket was a wicker basket with the top open, and he was getting out various containers of food.

A picnic.

Maude usually had picnics by herself—if you could call eating an apple beside the waterfall a picnic—and preferred it that way, since it allowed her to bask in the forest silence and peace in way she couldn't if anyone else was around.

So it was strange to feel a little shock of pleasure to find him sitting on a blanket, arranging containers of food, and she wasn't sure why. She was hungry admittedly, so the food was welcome, but it was clear that sex wasn't on the menu—or maybe not straight away—and that was unexpected.

He looked up as she approached and his mouth curved, and the smile he gave her was so warm and so unbelievably attractive, it felt as if her heart had turned a somersault.

'Afternoon, nymph,' he said and then gestured to the food. 'Polly made far too much lunch so, of course, I thought you might like to share a picnic with me.'

Not many people in Maude's life had ever done anything for her. Not her mother and not her grandparents. Her mother had remembered the odd birthday, and her grandparents had at least made sort of an effort for Christmas, but generally she had been expected to follow the rules and look after herself.

That Dominic had decided to put on a picnic for her, and at her favourite place in the woods, made her chest go tight for a second.

'Oh,' she said, trying hard to ignore how that tightness had crept into her throat. 'This is…lovely.'

He patted the blanket next to him. 'Sit and I'll get you something to eat. It's all pregnancy friendly, I made sure.'

She settled down on the blanket where he'd indicated, sudden anxiety clutching at her. 'Did you tell Polly about—?'

'No, I didn't.' His dark eyes searched her face. 'Not yet anyway. Are you worried about people knowing?'

She didn't want to be worried, and yet she still hadn't told anyone and she supposed there was a reason for that. A reason she hadn't wanted to talk about it with anyone else yet.

'I suppose I am,' she said after a moment. 'My grandparents at least. They're very old-fashioned and very strict. Mum was a single mother and they didn't like that, so I'm very sure they won't like me being one either.'

He took a delicious-looking sandwich out of a container, put in on a plate, then handed the plate to her. 'Why do you care?' he asked. 'It's your life and being a single mother isn't an issue these days.'

Good point. She didn't know why she cared. It wasn't as if they'd been very understanding of her growing up. They'd tried to do their best for her, she knew that, but still. They'd taken her from her mother on the pretext of wanting to give her a better life, yet she hadn't been happy. Apparently happiness wasn't included in a better life.

'They promised me a piece of land as a rewilding project,' she said, picking up the sandwich. 'And I'm pretty sure if they find out I'm pregnant, they'll change their minds about giving it to me.'

He gave her an enigmatic look. 'You can find a piece of land anywhere to rewild. You don't need that one, do you?'

She took a bite out of the sandwich and chewed slowly. It was indeed as delicious as it looked. 'It's a gift,' she said after she'd swallowed her food. 'I don't have money enough to buy my own.'

Dominic's gaze remained enigmatic.

He was casual today, in black jeans and a loose sweatshirt the same deep green as the forest behind him. The colour suited his olive skin and the deep, dark brown of his eyes. He looked on the surface like a civilised man having a picnic in the grass and yet there was another man who looked out from behind his eyes. Passionate, raw. Possessive and feral almost.

The man he was in her bed every night.

She could see that man now, glittering in the blackness of his eyes. In the subtle curve of his mouth. In the long-fingered hand he had propped on his knee. In the crackling electricity of his presence.

It made her want to know more about him, the reasons Dominic kept him so locked down.

'Ah, yes,' he said. 'Money is an issue. But there are solutions to that.'

Maude stared at him in surprise. 'Solutions? What solutions?'

Again he smiled, as if he knew a delicious secret that she didn't. 'I've been thinking.' He reached for a bottle of fresh orange juice and poured her some in a plastic glass, then handed it to her.

'Oh, dear,' she muttered, taking the glass. 'You thinking is never good.'

He laughed, the sound rich and full of genuine amusement. 'There aren't many people in the world who get to say that kind of thing to me.'

'Well, maybe there should be more,' she said, unable to resist smiling back, feeling oddly pleased with herself that she'd made him laugh. 'You could do with being taken down a peg or two.'

He laughed again and shook his head. 'You're not afraid of me at all, are you?'

She gave him a look over the top of her glass as she sipped her juice. 'Should I be?'

'Many people are. I'm very rich and quite powerful, you see.' He poured some orange juice for himself. 'I'm surprised you weren't that night in the woods. I was a stranger to you, after all.'

'You were, but...I wasn't afraid. It was the forest. It has a...power. At least, to me it does.' She bit her lip, wondering why she was telling him this. Her feelings about the forest always sounded stupid when she told people aloud, and they always looked at her strangely.

But Dominic was looking at her now with interest, not hiding his curiosity. 'A power?' he asked. 'What kind of power?'

'It sounds weird and you'll probably laugh.'

'I won't laugh.' His gaze didn't flicker and he wasn't smiling now. He meant it.

She let out a breath. 'At the commune, Mum wasn't around a lot, so I was left on my own. I used to hang out in the commune garden because I loved the flowers and the plants, and the woman who managed the garden would tell me what each plant was and what it was used for. But when she wasn't there, I'd run into the forest on the border of the commune. I felt as if the trees were...watching over me. As if they were protecting me.' She'd looked away as she'd said it, not wanting to meet his gaze, yet she couldn't help glancing at him now. 'It's weird, yes.'

But he wasn't laughing. He was looking at her in a very intent way, making all the breath go out of her. 'It's not weird,' he said. 'There were no other children there?'

'A couple of babies, but no, no one my age.'

'So, you were lonely.'

It wasn't a question and a small jolt of shock hit her. Was she that easy to read? 'What makes you say that?' she asked, cagily. 'I never said I was lonely.'

'You didn't have to.' His tone was matter-of-fact. 'An only child with no parent watching over them?' He let the question hang for a moment then went on, 'And I know this because my father used to do the same with me. He would leave me at the manor for weeks at a time, with no one here to watch over me.'

Maude was momentarily diverted. 'You were? And you had no one?'

'There was Craddock, the gamekeeper, who lived in the cottage you're living in now. He used to take me hunting.' There was an odd note in Dominic's voice that she couldn't quite interpret. 'I'll tell you a secret. I was always terrified of the forest.'

Maude blinked. 'You? Terrified?'

'Oh, yes.' The corner of his mouth had curved, but it didn't look like amusement. 'My father used to—' He broke off, and Maude was conscious of a sudden tension around him that hadn't been there before.

This was painful for him. She could tell that right away.

'Don't feel you have to tell me if you don't want

to,' she said quietly. 'Just because I told you something about me.'

Dominic looked down at his plate and the sandwich sitting on it, remaining silent for a time. Then he said, 'My father turned me out at night a couple of times. Made me sleep in the forest. I had to "face my fear".' He glanced at her suddenly, his eyes full of an intense expression she couldn't quite read. 'He said that if you didn't control your fear, it would end up controlling you, and I suppose he was right.' He smiled, but it didn't reach his eyes. 'After the first couple of nights, I wasn't afraid of the forest any more.'

But Maude could hear the lie in his voice. Was it really the forest he'd been afraid of? Or was it his father perhaps? He'd mentioned that his childhood hadn't been a happy one...

'You must have hated your grandparents then,' Dominic went on before she could speak. 'Taking you away from your mother and the commune.'

It was a clear change of subject, and Maude decided not to press him about it. Certainly not if it was painful for him.

'They weren't easy people,' she admitted. 'But I didn't hate them. They only wanted what was best for me.'

'Sounded like being left in the commune was what was best for you,' he said evenly. 'Did they even ask you if you wanted to go? And what did your mother have to say about any of it?'

She met his dark gaze, feeling oddly defensive of her grandparents, even though that was what she'd always thought herself. 'They didn't ask, no. And my mother had nothing to say about it. If I'd stayed there, I wouldn't have had an education.'

'Ah.' He raised his glass and took a sip. 'So you preferred being with your grandparents, then?'

'That's what was best for me in the end.'

'That's not what I asked.' His dark gaze was disturbingly intense. 'I asked if you preferred being with them over the commune.'

She didn't like the question and how unsure and defensive it made her feel. As if she'd had a choice about whether to go with her grandparents or stay at Earthsong with her mother, which she hadn't.

'Does it matter?' she said, trying to sound casual. 'It was a long time ago.'

But that unnerving black gaze of his seemed to see right inside her. 'I didn't ask to make you uncomfortable. I only asked because it's clear you love the forest here at Darkfell. And I wondered if you'd like to stay beyond the term of your contract.'

Maude stared back at him in shock. 'Stay?'

'Yes. Make the position permanent, so to speak.'

'But you said you were going to sell the place after the baby is born.'

'I did. And then I changed my mind.'

Carefully, Maude put down her plastic cup and clasped her hands together, trying to keep the sudden fearful hope inside her. 'You're serious?' She searched his face. 'You really want me to stay on here?'

'Yes, I'm serious. However…' He paused and she saw

it again, the flash of iron in his gaze, making her heart tighten. 'There are strings attached.'

Her heart tightened still further. Of course there were. There were always strings with him.

'What strings?' she asked, unable to hide the wariness in her voice.

Dominic's dark eyes glittered. 'I want you to marry me, Maude.'

Dominic watched the shock blossom over Maude's lovely face, which he'd expected. He hadn't exactly been open with her about his idea.

He'd also been wanting to give her some space. It was why he hadn't gone to her cottage the moment he'd arrived. She was a wild creature, he'd decided, and with wild creatures you had to go slow. So he'd let her get used to him being around and only on the third night had he gone to her door.

He'd been meaning only to talk or to suggest, but then she'd thrown herself into his arms and that had been the end of that.

He'd spent every night in her bed since then, leaving in the early morning before she woke up, still wanting to give her that space. But he'd been thinking, over the course of the week, of the future and what would happen after their son was born.

It was real to him now, a future he'd never thought he'd want unrolling before him. But he did want it. He did. And he wanted her, too.

Marriage didn't mean much to him, since it hadn't

meant anything to his parents. His mother had been his father's lover and she'd left him not long after Dominic had turned two. He had no memories of her. Yet he'd decided that his son should have what he hadn't, a mother and a father, and what better way to tie it all together than to be married?

The idea hadn't bothered him as much as he'd thought it would. In fact, he liked it. Liked the thought of Maude being his wife. It would mean he'd be stuck with only one woman for the rest of his life, but he found he rather liked that thought too. It had been nearly a week and he still wanted her with as much hunger as he had that first time. Their nights together were incendiary. Of course, over time, their passion would wane because it always did, and then they might have to have a discussion about finding other partners, discreetly of course.

Until then though, he didn't see any reason why not to make her his wife. There were certain legal protections she would enjoy and she'd certainly like to stay here in the forest. They could keep their own lives as they were doing right now... Surely she wouldn't find it a problem?

Her warm brown eyes were wide with shock. 'Marry you?' she repeated huskily. 'But...why?'

'It would give you some legal protection,' he said easily. 'But more importantly, it would give our son a family.'

'He already has a family.'

'A family who are together,' Dominic clarified.

She was still staring at him, shock echoing in her gaze. 'But…you don't love me. And I don't love you.'

He almost laughed. 'Of course not. But that's not the kind of marriage I was thinking of.'

She didn't look at all reassured. 'So what kind of marriage were you thinking of?'

'Our lives would go on as they are now. I'll live in the manor and you'll live in the cottage. We will continue to sleep together and, I have to admit, that's another string, because I'm not staying celibate. You will have our son and he will continue to live here with both his parents.'

Maude frowned. 'I…'

'Nothing will change.' He made his voice as reassuring as he could, because now that he'd put the idea to her, he realised he very much wanted her to say yes. 'You will have your life and I will have mine. The only difference from now is that you can stay on here as the groundskeeper.'

'I still don't understand,' she said. 'If nothing will change, then why do we have to get married?'

Irritation wound through him, but he quelled it. Getting annoyed wouldn't help his case here.

'Why shouldn't we?' he said. 'It would be better for you financially, and, as I already said, would give you some legal protection if anything happens to me.'

'I mean…' Her gaze narrowed in that wary, suspicious way he was coming to dislike intensely. 'What are you getting out of it?'

He reached out and idly pushed a strand of golden hair back behind her ear, relishing the feel of the silky strands against his fingertips. 'I am getting you. In my bed every night with any luck.'

'But you have that already.'

'Except you will be my wife.'

'How is that different?'

Questions. She was all about questions. He couldn't resent that, though. She wanted to know and he liked that she had no qualms about asking.

'I've decided that I want a family,' he said, the truth coming out of his mouth before he'd even thought about it. 'I did think I'd never marry or have children, and I'd never wanted to. But now I'm going to be a father, I want to give my child the best start in life, and that's with a family.'

'Is it?' There was a crease between her brows. 'My grandparents were married and I didn't have a particularly good life with them.'

'So you had a better life with your mother?' he couldn't help saying. 'Who wasn't around, which made you lonely enough to go into the forest to find companionship?'

She flushed. 'That's not… It wasn't…'

'Nymph.' He reached for her hands and took them in his, because fighting like this wasn't going to help either of them. 'What are you so afraid of?'

She'd asked him that once, as he'd tried to resist her physically, still wanting to control his hunger for her, and he'd hated the question. But he had no qualms about turning it on her, since it was clear that the idea of marriage disturbed her and he didn't want it to.

She didn't pull her hands away, letting them rest in his, and he brushed his thumbs across her skin, wanting to soothe her, ease away her fears, whatever they were.

'I don't want…to be tied down,' she said haltingly, as if the words were difficult. 'I don't want to feel like I'm with my grandparents again, where I wasn't allowed to do anything or go anywhere. I had to be quiet, sit still, and not cause a fuss.'

He could understand that. It reminded him of his own childhood, bound by his father's rules, his behaviour forced into something that had never been natural to him. And, God, he'd told her about those nights in the forest, alone. He hadn't meant to, not when it exposed such a weakness in him. Yet still, he'd told her.

'I understand,' he said. 'But it won't be like that, I promise you. It'll be a legal marriage and that's all. You won't have to do anything or be anyone but yourself. Call it a whim of mine.' Her fingertips felt cold in his so he rubbed them gently. 'You can stay here. You won't have to leave. And when we tell people about the child, you can call me your husband. There'll be some surprise, because of my reputation, of course, but marrying me will make the announcement easier.'

She was nodding, but there was still a tightness around her eyes and her mouth, so he tugged her gently into his lap. She didn't protest as he put his arms around her, holding her, and it came to him, slowly, that though he'd held her before, he'd never held her like this. As a comfort rather than anything more.

He'd never felt the need to comfort anyone before or

even made any kind of comforting gesture. Why should he? When no one had comforted him? And he was surprised how good it made him feel when she turned her head into his neck, accepting the warmth of his body and the strength of his arms.

'You're a wild thing, nymph,' he murmured softly into her hair. 'And I know that I need to be careful with wild things. I won't cage you, understand? But also know one thing. I will be your forest. When you're lonely and need someone to look after you, don't go into the woods. Come to me instead.'

She looked up at him, her brown eyes dark, and he couldn't have said what she was thinking. Then she lifted a hand to his hair, her touch light. 'Badger,' she said softly.

His heart tightened in his chest at the tender sound in her voice. The press called him all kinds of things, and he'd never paid any attention to them, but this… This was a name she'd given him and he rather thought she was owed.

'Logically I should be "satyr", since you're my nymph,' he pointed out.

She wrinkled her nose. 'No, I like badger better. Also, you're not being particularly satyr-like now.'

'I can be if you'd rather.'

Her fingers sifted gently through his hair, her mouth curving as she looked up into his eyes. 'That night you were the god of the forest. And I let you catch me.'

Strange, mysterious woman. Wild and passionate one

minute, stubborn and angry the next, then warm and almost tender the minute after that.

She intrigued him.

She'll be your wife if she agrees.

The thought gripped him tight as a wave of possessiveness swamped him. Yes, she would be *his* wife. No one else's, just his.

'You did.' He tried not to let the possessiveness bleed into his voice. 'And you know what that means.'

Slowly, like the dawn breaking, she smiled. 'No. What?'

'It means you're mine.' This time he couldn't stop that possessiveness from colouring his voice. 'And the god of the forest always keeps what's his.'

He thought she might protest at his blatant declaration of ownership, but she didn't. Instead her eyes darkened further, the gold eclipsed. Did she like it? Did she want to be claimed?

He stared down at her, and it came to him then that it was a fine line she walked. Because yes, she did want that. Her mother hadn't wanted her, and her grandparents hadn't either. They'd taken her away, but it hadn't been about her, he thought. It had been for themselves, because they hadn't liked the way her mother had brought her up.

But that night, she'd let him catch her, because deep in her heart she wanted to be captured. She wanted to be held. Even though she fought against it and wanted her freedom, she also wanted that tether.

He wasn't sure why what she wanted mattered to

him, perhaps it was merely that she was carrying their child. Regardless, he wanted to give that to her. Both the tether and the freedom.

And why not? When it suits what you want very well.

There was an element of snideness in the thought, but he dismissed it. Yes, it worked well for what he wanted too, but who cared? In the end, they both got an arrangement that suited both their needs.

Maude clearly liked the thought of him keeping her, because her fingers tightened in his hair, bringing his head slowly lower until their lips met.

Her mouth was warm and she tasted both tart and sweet from the orange juice she'd been drinking, and he could feel the autumn sun on the back of his neck, as soft and warm as her mouth and body.

'Here,' he murmured, easing her down onto the blanket. 'Let me have you here. I've caught you, nymph, so you have to give me whatever I want.'

She was still smiling, but there was a delicate flush to her cheeks now, a sure sign of arousal. 'Do I?' There was a playful note in her voice. 'And what is it you want, O great god?'

He was already pulling at her clothing, and usually he was more adept, but he felt oddly desperate and inexplicably clumsy, and so she had to help him. She laughed as she got tangled in her jeans and underwear, until he covered her mouth with his, taking her laughter for himself.

Finally they were naked and he was stretched out above her, where he preferred to be, looking down at her, this beautiful, wild, uncanny woman he'd found in the forest that night, and he felt himself teetering on the edge of a cliff he hadn't known was there. But the feeling made no sense, so he kissed her again, relishing the way she arched beneath him, letting him know she wanted more, and then her legs wrapped around his waist and that was the sweetest feeling yet.

He guided himself into her, loving how she gasped as he pushed in slow, deep, and then he stopped, buried inside her. He lifted her hands and threaded her fingers through his, before pressing them down on the blanket, on either side of her head.

She smiled. 'I like you like this,' she said softly, her voice husky with pleasure. 'Naked and in the sun. You look like you're meant to be here. Like me.'

He shifted his hips, unable to look away, trapped by the pleasure darkening her eyes as he moved. 'Do I?' he asked, rough and raw. 'Like a god, if I remember right.'

She gave a soft laugh that ended on a gasp as he drew out of her, then slid deep inside again. 'Oh…yes…' She sighed. 'You are, badger.'

He found himself smiling back at her, staring into her eyes, gone molten and soft with liquid gold. 'Don't kill the moment, nymph.'

She laughed again, a soft sexy little laugh that had him kissing her, wanting to taste the joyous sound of it and keep it inside him. He couldn't remember the last time he'd smiled at someone during sex. The last time it had been playful, and teasing, and tender.

He rolled suddenly onto his back, just for a change, so she was above him, the sun turning her hair into a golden glory. Her face was alight, her hands braced on his chest, and when he gripped her hips, moving her, she sighed, her inner muscles squeezing him.

Beautiful nymph. Beautiful Maude.

A groan escaped him as she tilted her hips slightly. 'You're killing me,' he murmured, the pleasure sharper, hotter. 'I like it. Do it again.'

So she did, and he growled, making her laugh yet again, her body shaking on top of his. 'Animal,' she breathed. 'You're my favourite kind.'

He was rapidly losing the ability to think, but he paused again, deep inside, tightening his fingers on her hips. 'I'm your favourite kind of animal?'

'I like a badger.' She rocked against him. 'Move.'

'What?' He pretended to look surprised. 'Me? Move? Move where?'

Another laugh and she bent forward, her hair a golden curtain around them. 'Make me come, O great god,' she whispered against his mouth, 'and I'll be your slave for ever.'

'Oh, well, in that case…' He gripped her harder, moving beneath her, watching the teasing light in her eyes slowly fade, replaced by the burning pleasure that they always experienced with each other.

And even though she was above him, he had the oddest impression that he was the one falling. Falling into her brilliant golden eyes.

'You haven't said yes, Maude,' he whispered.

Her gaze was shadowed russet edged with gold. Darkness and light. Midnight and midsummer. The wild part of her and the joy. She kissed him, giving him a nip. 'Yes,' she whispered.

Then everything fell away and there was nothing in the world but the pleasure and the fire that ended it.

CHAPTER TEN

THREE DAYS LATER Maude stood in front of the little mirror in the cottage and stared at herself in the simple, gold silk shift dress. It was cut on the bias, hugging her breasts, hips and little bump, before flowing out into a gold swirl around her ankles. A beautiful dress. Her wedding dress.

She still found it hard to believe that she'd agreed to marry Dominic, especially considering her first thought when he'd asked her was an immediate no. And not because she had strong feelings about marriage itself—her grandparents admittedly hadn't seemed all that happy in theirs, yet Polly and John clearly were—but because she didn't want to feel bound to anyone. To be constrained by their rules and their expectations. She'd moved on from that when she'd moved out of her grandparents' house, but it hadn't been until she'd come to Darkfell that she'd felt truly free. She didn't want to give that up, not for anyone.

But Dominic had been adamant that nothing would change between them and she believed him. He hadn't given her a reason to doubt him since he'd decided to live here so why shouldn't she?

It had still been a deal for him—he'd made no secret of that—and while she felt an odd pinch of hurt for absolutely no reason, mostly she found that reassuring. No feelings were involved, it was still a business decision, and that she was comfortable with.

Taking his name for the sake of legal protection for her and the baby had even sounded logical, and if it meant they could both carry on as they had, with him in her bed when she wanted it, why shouldn't she?

It also took some of the pressure off when it came to explaining about the pregnancy. There would be questions, naturally, about how she came to marry such an infamous playboy, but at least she didn't need to say that her baby was the result of a night spent with a stranger in the forest.

Speaking of which, the others need to know.

Yes, the Your Girl Friday team really did. She'd been cagey on their usual Zoom calls, and while she'd had a few assessing looks, no one had asked her outright what was going on. They respected her need for space, which she appreciated.

She'd tell them later, after the wedding maybe. They'd be unhappy she hadn't let them know about either the baby or Dominic earlier, but too bad. It was her secret to keep for the time being.

Dominic, however, had insisted that Polly and John be told, and that the announcement should be made with her presence. She'd been reluctant, worrying a little about what the Harrises would think of her pregnancy and then her forthcoming marriage. But they hadn't been judgemental. In fact, they'd been thrilled, Polly even going so far as to give both her and Dominic a hug.

She hadn't expected that and it was relieving. It made her wonder why she'd been worried about it at all. Probably leftover anxiety from her grandparents' judgemental upbringing.

Carefully, she picked up the length of sheer golden silk that was her veil, and put it on her head. She'd chosen the gown and veil from a website the day after she'd agreed to be Dominic's wife and he'd had them shipped to Darkfell. He'd also asked her what she preferred in terms of a ceremony and, since she had no strong feelings about it, having never thought she'd ever marry, she'd only shrugged. He'd nodded and then asked her if she minded him organising it, which she didn't. He'd surprise her, he'd said, which could have been a little worrying, but she felt oddly calm about letting him do it. He'd never do anything she wouldn't want. She felt that in her bones.

Stepping out of the cottage, Maude was surprised to see a lit torch standing in the ground outside the front door, flaring in the sunshine. An arrow on the ground, formed of sticks, pointed in the direction of the forest, and a crown of woven leaves and flowers sat in the grass beside it.

A strange little feeling gripped her tight, though she couldn't have said what it was, a wave of the strangest warmth. She found herself smiling as she went over to the arrow and picked up the crown. It was competently woven, the leaves fresh and green, the wildflowers bright. It was obviously for her.

Her throat felt tight for some reason and the warmth in her chest expanded. Dominic had done this and he'd put thought into it. He'd considered her, considered what was important to her, what she liked, and he'd made an effort. This marriage might be only a business deal, but he'd made it special.

Is marrying him really such a good idea?

Maude ignored both the thought and the tight feeling in her throat. She'd said she'd marry him and she would, and it wouldn't change their arrangement. It was for the baby anyway, and the baby was far more important than her own feelings.

She put the crown of leaves and flowers on her head, over the veil, then turned in the direction of the arrow and walked into the forest. There were more torches and arrows, pointing the way, and she soon realised where she was being directed. It made the warmth inside her glow brighter.

She moved deeper into the trees, mindful of her dress, until she came to the little path that led to the forest waterfall and pool, because of course that was where he'd directed her.

Her special place. And since the day she'd agree to marry him, where she'd sat astride him, naked and free, and brought them both to the ultimate pleasure, it had become *their* special place.

She stepped out of the trees and into the clearing,

her heart thumping, that strange, warm feeling moving through her, to find Dominic standing beside the pool, waiting for her. Another man stood there smiling, obviously a priest, and Polly and John were also there. Witnesses.

Not that she saw anyone but Dominic.

The autumn sun had blessed them today, shining down onto the clearing and onto him. Tall and powerful. He was dressed in black trousers and a simple black shirt, but on his head was also a crown of leaves. His black hair gleamed like spilled ink in the sunlight, the white stripe almost glowing amidst the green of the leaves. His eyes were as dark as his hair, and he didn't smile.

But when he looked at her, she felt something inside her bloom.

This man, who hadn't laughed at her when she'd told him about how connected she felt to the trees and to nature. Who'd accepted both her stubbornness and her passion, her fire and her wild spirit, and hadn't punished her for any of it. Who hadn't forced her to be anyone but herself. And who'd created this beautiful ceremony just for her, taking all the things that she found important, and turning them into the most perfect moment.

Everything about this was for her and so was he.

He was the god of the forest and she was his chosen queen.

She walked slowly over to him, her heart feeling somehow larger and fuller in her chest, the warm feeling flowing through her and almost bringing tears to her eyes, making her throat ache.

He reached out to her and clasped her hand, his fingers threading through hers. 'Surprise,' he murmured. 'I hope this is adequate.'

She gripped his hand tightly, swallowing past the lump in her throat. 'Adequate? It's…perfect. Just perfect.'

His dark gaze roved over her hungrily. 'And so are you.'

She flushed with pleasure then reached up to touch his crown. 'Who made these?'

'I did.' He smiled then and it lit his face like the sun shining down on them. 'It wasn't as easy as I'd hoped.'

'I love them.' The warm feeling in her heart grew, putting down roots and sprouting new leaves.

'Good.' He gripped her hand tight. 'Are you ready?'

Are you? You're afraid.

No, she wasn't. Not of him, not of this. And this powerful feeling growing inside her was nothing. Simple pleasure at how he'd made this day so special. It was nothing more than that.

It's not and you know it.

But Maude ignored the thought, nodding at Dominic and then turning to face the priest.

It wasn't a long ceremony, but, try as she might, she couldn't ignore that feeling inside her as it grew and bloomed, wrapping strong roots around her heart and binding it tight.

When it was her turn to speak, the words were hoarse,

and when it was time to exchange rings, she looked down to see her own ring was shaped as a circlet of oak leaves, in white gold.

Her vision wavered, tears filling her eyes unexpectedly. He'd thought of every detail. He'd made this special, this ceremony that was supposed to be only a business deal. This ceremony that was only about legal protection, nothing more.

Her heart thumped even harder and it was difficult to catch a breath.

The priest was saying words and then Dominic gave her another ring, his ring, and that too was a circlet of oak leaves. She pushed it onto his finger almost automatically, the roots around her heart tightening still further, choking her.

Then she found herself looking up at Dominic as the priest continued to speak. The sun was behind his head, throwing his face into shadow, but his eyes gleamed, and in them she could see the man she'd given herself to that night in the forest. The fierce, passionate man, behind his urbane and polished front.

The man you've fallen in love with.

The thought wound through her head, the roots in her heart piercing it right through. Roots wrapping around her bones, growing down into her soul. An unbreakable connection, a tether she'd never be free of.

Dominic bent his head and kissed her, the priest naming them husband and wife.

No, she wasn't in love with him. She *wasn't*. She loved her friends and the forest, and her unborn child, but she didn't want to be in love with a man. And most especially not a man like him. He gave, she couldn't deny that, but he also demanded things in return. Her honesty, her passion, her time, her attention.

It wouldn't matter if she hadn't wanted to give him those things, but she had wanted to, so she did. Giving him small pieces of herself, not realising what was happening, not understanding what she was doing until it was too late.

Love had rooted itself so deep inside her she was never going to be able to cut it out.

Her fingers were cold, and Dominic must have felt them, because as he lifted his head, he frowned. 'Are you okay?' he asked, concern in his eyes.

'Oh, yes.' She quickly pulled her hand from his and pasted on a smile. 'I'm fine.'

She tried to ignore the feeling as she and Dominic received congratulations from Polly and John, before Dominic took her hand and led her back through the forest to the manor.

She didn't speak the whole way, her throat tight, her chest hurting. She was acutely conscious of her hand in his, of the ring of oak leaves circling her finger, and, try as she might, she couldn't ignore the feeling in her heart, strong and aching, binding itself with her soul.

Love had never been spoken of in her grandparents' house. No one had ever said to her 'I love you'. It was only ever 'for your own good' or 'we only want what's best for you'. Even Sonya hadn't said those words to her, not even when her grandparents had taken her away from Earthsong. Her mother hadn't even protested, leaving Maude to watch her walk away without a backwards look.

Once Maude had realised that they weren't going back to Earthsong, that the ice cream had been only a pretext to get her into the car, she'd wept all the way to her grandparents' house, an empty feeling in her heart. As if the most beautiful grove of trees had been growing there, but now they'd been cut down and the grove razed, the earth salted.

At her grandparents' house, there had been no wild forests for her to find comfort in. No garden of flowers. No herbs. No trees or even plants. There had been only a concreted space for her grandfather to park his car and that was it. Living there had killed something in Maude's soul.

She'd tried to make the best of it, since she'd had nowhere else to go, tried to be a good girl for her grandparents. School, with its playgrounds of concrete and metal, with timetables and bells, and rigid rules around behaviour, had been its own special hell. She'd tried there too, because her grandparents had given up their retirement to make sure she'd have a better start in life than what her mother could give her. They were doing it for her, they'd said.

Yet it had never felt as though they were doing it for her. It had felt as if she was a millstone around their necks that they'd had no choice but to deal with. And her mother, for all the freedom Sonya had given her, had made her feel that way too.

Maude had never been a child either her mother or her grandparents had wanted. She hadn't been a child at all. What she'd been was a rope around their necks, dragging them down.

You'll drag him down too.

Yes, she would. Eventually. He hadn't chosen her because he'd wanted her. He'd chosen her out of necessity. For their baby's sake. And knowing that really shouldn't hurt, since the baby was more important than either her or Dominic's feelings, and yet…

Maude fought to ignore the abruptly painful feeling in her heart as they came out of the forest and walked over the lawn to the manor. Dominic turned then, not making for the front door as she'd expected, but heading along the little brick path that led to the walled garden. And when she stepped through the stone doorway into it, the feeling inside her became even more painful, because a white silk pavilion had been erected near the pond in the middle, a table and chairs set out beneath it. On the table was food, drink, and the most perfect little wedding cake.

Maude stopped, her eyes suddenly full of tears.

He's done all this for you and you don't deserve it—not any of it.

Of course she didn't. She'd saddled him with a life he'd never wanted and now couldn't get out of.

She was the one tying *him* down. Not vice versa.

Dominic, slightly ahead of her and still holding her hand, turned. Then, obviously noticing the look on her face, frowned. 'Maude? What is it?'

She let go of his hand. 'I… I'm not feeling well.' The lie rolled off her tongue so smoothly it was as if she'd been lying all her life.

His expression became concerned and he stepped closer. 'You're not? How so?'

'Just a headache.' She clasped her hands together so he wouldn't seem them trembling. 'It's nothing.'

'It isn't nothing.' He reached for her clasped hands and pulled them gently apart, the warmth of his skin against her numb fingertips. 'Your fingers are cold.' His frown deepened. 'What's wrong?'

'It's nothing,' she repeated and tried to pull her hands away.

Except he held onto them. 'It's something,' he said quietly. 'It's not a headache, is it?'

Maude tried to get a breath, tried to think of another lie, but the way he was looking at her now, she knew he'd never believe her. It was as if he could see right inside her head, read her mind, know all her thoughts.

'I just…' She jerked her hands out of his and stepped back from him, putting some distance between them. 'What is this for?'

He made no effort to reach for her again, frowning. 'This? What do you mean this?'

'The ceremony. The crowns. The rings.'

His frown deepened. 'I thought you would like it.'

'But there's no reason for it.' Her heart ached and ached. She was ruining this, ruining this day he'd made perfect just for her, and she couldn't stop herself. 'It was only supposed to be a legal requirement. It didn't need to be…special.'

'It was for you,' he said, searching her face as if for clues. 'I thought you would appreciate it if we made it an occasion, and I thought it would be nice to have it in the forest with some things that were meaningful to you.'

You are ruining this by making a scene. Stop it.

Except she couldn't stop it. She couldn't seem to stem the words that were pouring out of her mouth. 'I didn't ask you to do it for me. I didn't ask you to make it special. And what about you? Why wasn't there anything meaningful to you in there too? Why did it have to be all about me?'

Dominic stared at the woman in front of him, so startlingly beautiful in her golden gown and crowned with leaves.

His wood nymph. His wife.

He didn't know what had gone wrong, but something had. Somehow, in the moment between when they'd said their vows and walked back to the manor, something had changed. Something had spooked this wild creature of his and he had no idea what it was.

He'd taken great pleasure in organising the ceremony, he had to admit. He'd put the kind of thought into it that he'd never put into anything but his business, and he wasn't sure why, but he had. It had felt important to create something that Maude would like, since he was the one who'd suggested the idea of marriage in the first place, and for it to be special for her, because he didn't want her to regret it.

When she'd stepped out of the forest, resplendent in gold, wearing the leaf crown he'd made, he'd felt the most acute pleasure that this beautiful, mysterious woman was now his. A pleasure that had only deepened when he'd put his ring on her finger, the possessive part of him roaring its satisfaction.

She was his wife now and she was pregnant with their child, and he would keep them, protect them, make sure nothing would hurt them.

He'd been looking forward to cutting the cake and eating the food Polly had prepared, and talking about their future and planning it together. Then, later, taking her to his bed in the manor for a change, and making her his wife in every way possible.

She'd looked a touch pale as they'd walked away from the pool and her fingers had been cold in his, it was true. But he hadn't thought she'd suddenly and angrily demand to know why he'd made the ceremony so special, or why it was all about her.

There was something else going on here, he was sure.

He studied her face for a moment. 'This isn't about the wedding, is it? Something's upset you.'

She was pale in the sun, all the warmth leached from her brown eyes. If he didn't know any better, he would have said she was afraid, though he couldn't think what she'd be afraid of. He'd promised not to sell Darkfell, and he'd also told her that things wouldn't change between them, so what else was it?

'You don't love me, do you?' she asked suddenly.

Frowning at the abrupt question, he reached out and grabbed her, his hands on her silken hips, pulling her close, as if that would make understanding what this was about easier. 'No. Love was never going to be a part of this, I already told you that.'

Despite the wild look in her eyes, her body was already softening against his, moulding itself to him. Recognising him the way his body recognised hers. 'Good,' she said, her hands coming to his chest the way they always did, as if she couldn't stop herself from touching him. 'I love our child, but…not you.'

The words felt like small slivers of glass pushed slowly beneath his skin and he wasn't sure why. Because he didn't want her to love him. He didn't want anyone to love him. Love demanded things, required things. Love was a list of expenses that he had to pay back. Love was a deal impossible to negotiate with. Love was an empty house and loneliness.

He didn't want that again, not for himself. He never had.

'Just as well,' he said evenly. 'Because I don't love you either.'

'But our child? You'll love him, won't you?'

Tension crept through him, making his muscles tight and his jaw ache. It was true, his heart had died the death of a thousand cuts. His father's cold words and his efforts to 'harden him up'. Little by little the store of love he'd had inside him had leaked away until there was nothing left.

Until he'd hardened himself entirely just as his father had wanted him to. As hard as his father had been. No, harder.

His father had turned him into the perfect business-man, the perfect CEO, and yet he'd retained enough of his 'soft' nature, as his father had termed it, to make it clear he wasn't a carbon copy.

It wasn't soft to enjoy pleasure, and so he'd cultivated it as carefully as he'd cultivated his business acumen, until finally he was both the businessman and the syb-arite, because why not? Why couldn't you have your cake and eat it too?

Why couldn't you have all that, *and* love your child? None of it was mutually exclusive. He didn't need a heart in order to love. All he needed was to not be his father, and he'd already achieved that.

'Of course, I'll love him.' And to make the point, he smoothed his hand over her bump where their baby lay. 'He's my son.'

Abruptly, as if his touch had burned her, she pulled herself out of his arms, and took a couple of steps away.

He stared at her in surprise. 'Maude? What the hell is going on?'

'Your childhood,' she said, ignoring him. 'Why was it unhappy?'

'What's that got to do with anything?'

'If you want to be a good father to your child, then I want to know why you were so unhappy as a kid. So we can avoid making the same mistakes.'

Impatience twisted inside him. He had no idea where

she was going with this, or what had provoked it, and he really didn't want to continue the conversation. What he wanted to do was cut their cake and then take her to bed.

'Later,' he said, trying to temper his tone. 'Let's have some cake first at least.'

'No,' she said, oddly insistent. 'Now. I need to know who I married.'

He took a calming breath, trying to hold onto his temper, because she was clearly upset so maybe going along with this—whatever it was—would finally get him to the truth.

'Fine.' He thrust his hands into the pockets of his trousers so he wouldn't keep reaching for her, since clearly she didn't want him to. 'What do you want to know?'

She'd folded her arms across her chest as if cold. 'Everything.'

'Okay. Well, my mother was my father's lover. They weren't married. She walked out when I was two. My father was going to put me up for adoption because he'd never wanted children, but then he changed his mind. He decided he needed an heir after all and, lo, there I was.' The words had a bitter tinge to them, but he decided he didn't care. He *was* bitter and he had reason to be. 'Dad wanted a strong businessman for a son, so from an early age that's how he treated me. Everything I wanted, I had to negotiate for. Clothes, food, heating, toys, his attention, his time. Nothing came for free. I had to pay for it all.

'When I was thirteen, I was handed a list of expenses

I'd incurred merely by existing and he expected me to pay him back.' He kept his tone casual, because, after all, while he might be bitter, all of this had happened many years ago and it had no bearing on what was happening now. 'My father wanted me to learn how to be a boardroom warrior, how to be hard, to never let anything get in the way of a good deal, and that was his way of doing things. He told me that if I paid back the money he spent on my upbringing, I'd be named his heir.'

Maude was silent, her golden-brown eyes fixed on his.

'He died of a heart attack when I was seventeen,' he went on. 'But I hadn't paid him back yet—nearly, I was very close—so I missed out on being named as his heir. I suspect the game had always been rigged and he'd never intended to leave it to me anyway. I just didn't know it until then.'

Her gaze flickered, though what she was thinking he didn't know. 'What did you do?' she asked.

'I took the company back.' He smiled, though it was rather more savage than he'd meant it to be. 'I put into practice every lesson he'd ever taught me, and I fought the board of Lancaster Developments into submission. Then I took the company apart, piece by little piece, and sold all of it. Then with that money I started my own company, and built it so that it was larger than his ever was.' He'd always found some satisfaction in that, yet saying it out loud to Maude now, it almost sounded... petty. 'You could say that my father would have been proud of me,' he went on, ignoring the feeling, 'because

I turned myself into him. Everything I learned I put to good use as a businessman and he wasn't wrong about a lot of things.'

There was a taut expression on her face. 'Will you teach the baby those same lessons?'

It was a fair question, though he hated she'd felt the need to even ask it. 'No,' he said fiercely. 'I will never do to him what my father did to me. Never.'

The tension in her face had eased slightly, yet something was still wrong, he knew it.

'Is that what was worrying you?' he asked. 'You'd think I'd hurt our—'

'No,' she interrupted quickly. 'No, I don't think that, not at all. It's just... Well, I suppose we both have our issues, and I'm not going to be the usual kind of wife. So if you're expecting me to be a certain thing...' She trailed off, but he didn't need her to explain.

He'd been right, she *had* been afraid, and he could understand why. Her life with her grandparents had left its mark on her and she was worried he might do the same thing to her. He wouldn't, of course. All he expected of her was that she be the delightful creature she already was.

'I'm not expecting you to be anything but yourself, nymph,' he said gently, and when he took his hand out of his pocket and extended it to her, it was in invitation rather than as a demand. 'Come and sit down with me. Let's eat this wedding breakfast and talk about anything you want. Or not talk if that's your preference.'

For a long moment she stared at him, as if she were

a wild creature unsure of whether to trust him or not. Then slowly she came to him and took his hand, and together they sat under the white silk pavilion and ate their wedding breakfast.

He told her about the forest and Craddock, and the stag he'd cried over. 'My father sneered at me,' he said, sipping on his glass of champagne. '"It's just a dumb animal", he told me. "If you can't handle shooting a deer, then how are you going to survive in the business world?"'

'Your father was the dumb animal, not you.' Maude's dark eyes were full of fire. 'What a terrible thing to say.'

'It was,' he agreed. 'Dad only had terrible things to say.' It didn't feel bad to talk to her about these moments of vulnerability. In fact, it felt as if he could tell her anything, anything at all. 'You should know,' he continued, after a moment's pause, 'that I haven't led a good life, nymph. Nothing was more important than my own pleasure, and even that was getting dull. At least until the night of the bacchanal.'

She leaned her elbows on the table, velvety eyes dark. 'So, what changed?'

He looked at her. 'You know what changed. You, being in the woods that night too. You, running from me. You, giving me all your passion even though I was a stranger to you.' He paused, because this was a confession that felt dangerous somehow, and yet he had to say it. 'You changed my life that night, Maude.'

Something flickered in her gaze, an expression gone

too fast for him to read. But then she leaned forward and reached for his hand where it rested on the tabletop, her long, slender fingers twining with his. He hadn't asked for any of her confidences, so when she spoke, everything in him went still.

'When my gran came to get me from the commune, Mum walked away,' Maude said slowly. 'And she never looked back. Not even for one last glimpse of me. She just walked away as if I meant nothing to her.'

There was pain in her eyes as she spoke and he could see how deeply this had hurt her.

He stroked his thumb over the back of her hand. 'I'm sorry,' he said, which was pitifully inadequate, but it was all he could think of to say. 'That's a terrible thing for a mother to do.'

'We should have swapped places.' A faint smile turned her mouth. 'I would have loved to sleep in the forest. Instead, all I got was my grandparents' concrete garden, with no trees, or flowers or grass.'

'Poor nymph,' he murmured, and he meant it. 'That must have been hell on earth for you.'

'It was,' she said simply. 'Leaving that place was the best thing I ever did.'

There was a silence then, of mutual acknowledgement of the hurts they'd both suffered.

Then he said, to break the moment, 'So where did you go after that?'

The conversation turned to less painful subjects, though no less interesting to him, as she told him about her life after she'd left her grandparents' house.

Then they talked about casual subjects, mundane things such as their favourite foods and their favourite books. The music they liked and the movies they'd enjoyed. He told her how he'd hiked to Everest base camp once when he'd been younger, and she told him that she'd always wanted to see the Amazon rainforest.

Then he asked her what it was that she actually did in his forest, and that was enough to make her grab his hand and lead him into the trees, talking all the while. She named trees and plants as she went, and what their niche in the forest ecology was, and how everything worked in concert with each other. And he saw it all with new eyes. Saw her anew too. Glowing with passion, bright with interest and curiosity. Nature was fiercely important to her, he could see, and she knew so much about it. Everything was connected, she told him, everything on this planet was connected.

Perhaps it was. When she talked like that, perhaps he even believed her. He certainly felt connected to her in a way he'd never experienced with another person.

They were in a little clearing with bracken on the ground when he stopped and reached for her. She'd been talking about ferns, but he was impatient now, because she was golden and glowing, and she was his wife. He wanted her and he was tired of waiting.

She didn't protest as he laid her down on the bracken, taking off her gown and veil, but leaving on her crown. As he left on his. Because they were both rulers of this little piece of land, king and queen of the forest, and this would be their marriage bed.

This time, though, he lay on his back, with her astride him, her hair a golden mane down her back, her hands braced on his chest. And he thought he'd died and gone to heaven. Because surely heaven was this, making love to a wood nymph who was his wife, on a bed of bracken, in a forest clearing.

And he realised, as she rose and fell above him, the pleasure twining around both of them, that this had gone beyond mere sex. Sex he knew very well, because he'd had a lot of it in his life. But this, what they were doing right now, right here, wasn't sex. It was more, it was deeper. It was reverent and sacred. It was worship.

It wasn't just about bodies. It was about souls.

He had no idea why he was thinking this, because he wasn't a man much given to poetry. But there was poetry in this. In her.

In her stubbornness and wild temper. In the joy she took in the things that were important to her. In the way her hand would rest on her bump every so often as if soothing the tiny baby inside her. In her touching his hair, warmth in her eyes, and calling him badger.

And in this, her gasps of pleasure, her eyes gone molten as he worshipped her, in the perfection of them moving together, slowly. Building this little castle of pleasure and wonder between them.

He'd never felt anything like it and he knew in that moment that he never would again. That for him it would always be this woman. That any other partner wouldn't be able to give him what she could. And he was at peace with that.

She was his wife and she would never leave him.

He'd make sure of it.

CHAPTER ELEVEN

Maude sat in the sitting room of the manor, sipping the hot chocolate Dominic had made for her. The fire crackled softly in the grate, warming the room.

It had been a week since the wedding and though she'd hoped the new ache in her heart would fade, it hadn't.

She should have left him in the walled garden the day she'd married him. She should have turned and walked out, but she hadn't. She'd tried to provoke an argument instead, wanting to use it to poison those roots growing around her heart, but he hadn't given her one.

He'd told her about his awful childhood and his terrible father and what his father had done to him and listening to his history had somehow made those roots stronger, not weaker.

No child should have had to live through that, and yet he had. He'd survived, even thrived, and in his own stubborn endurance, she'd seen herself.

They were the same. And while their childhoods had left their scars, they'd both come through the fire strong, and if not completely whole, then at least near enough to make no difference.

Then he'd made her show him the forest, listening as she'd talked about it, asking questions and being curious, inviting her passion about the forest to bloom. And it had.

Making love to him on the forest floor, the trees standing sentinel around them, had been one of the most pleasurable and spiritual experiences of her life.

She hadn't been able to leave him after that.

Learning more about him hadn't made her any less in love with him, and she didn't know what to do.

For the first couple of days, she'd looked for excuses to demand a divorce, or just to move away, but he hadn't given her any. As he'd promised, nothing changed. He came to the cottage at night and then left before she woke up the next day.

He'd mentioned something about a honeymoon, perhaps she might want to go to the Amazon? But she had a feeling that would only make her love him even more and so she'd put him off. He hadn't pushed.

She'd begun coming into the manor at night, usually to join him for dinner, and they'd spend a good couple of hours there, talking as they ate. He was interesting, had travelled to a lot of interesting places and done some interesting things, and she even found herself fascinated when he talked about some of the new startups he'd been an angel investor in. Plenty of them had been in eco technology, and she'd been surprised when he'd confessed that he wanted to put money into research for new tech that could help the planet and the poorer communities that lived on it.

He wasn't just some self-absorbed rich man at all. He had a good heart and he cared, and she loved him for it.

It was a problem, that love. She didn't know what to do about it.

He'd told her love wasn't a part of their marriage and she hadn't wanted it to be either, yet that made no difference to the feeling in her heart. She loved him all the same, and a part of her selfishly wanted him to love her in return.

Dominic came into the sitting room and sat down next to her, pulling her into his arms as he did so. He was very physically affectionate; she loved that about him too.

'You look pensive, nymph. Anything the matter?'

'No.'

A lie, of course. There was definitely something the matter, but she wasn't going to tell him what it was. He didn't need to know and while that selfish part of her wanted more, she had to ignore it. He didn't want love and she had no right to demand it from him.

You're being selfish, though. Lying to him because you can't bear to have that conversation. Because if you do, you'll lose him. Because you like keeping him tied to you without having to make any compromises yourself.

The thought whispered in her head, doubt eating away at her. It was true, wasn't it? She *was* being selfish. She was enjoying this marriage they'd entered into, where she could come and go as she pleased and have no demands placed on her, where she had him as well as all the freedom she wanted.

It was a business deal for him, and that made it okay, because then she wasn't a millstone around his neck, dragging him down.

Yet there was a small, painful, honest part of her that wasn't happy. That wanted more. That wanted that last little piece from him, to be loved as she loved him.

Except she could never ask for that, not without revealing how dishonest she'd been since the day she'd married him.

He'll never love you anyway, not when no one else did.

She shifted again, that knowledge like a barb sticking under her skin.

'There is something the matter,' Dominic said, looking down at her. 'What is it?'

Maude took a breath. She didn't want to upset the delicate balance they'd found together with the truth.

'I'm just thinking about the future,' she lied. 'And what it's going to look like.'

He frowned slightly. 'Our future, you mean?'

'Yes. You and I, and the baby. Will I still be in the cottage? Or will we be here? Or…what?'

Dominic shrugged. 'It's up to you. I promised you things wouldn't change and they haven't.'

'I know, but…the child is going to find it odd if we're still in separate places when he gets older.'

'It's hardly separate,' Dominic pointed out. 'It's still the same property.'

'Yes, but you've got a foot half in the city.'

'So? You wanted your own life, Maude.'

This was not the conversation she'd wanted to have, yet now her own lie had taken on a life of its own and she couldn't let it go. 'I know and I still want that. But… our child will have the life we give him, and I want to know what kind of life he'll have.'

Dominic's dark eyes narrowed. 'Are you imagining me leaving for months on end like my father did?'

'No, of course not. But…you'll still leave.'

'And then I'll come back. What's the problem?'

The problem is that I'll be here without you.

Except she couldn't say that. This was about their son and that was all. 'I… He'll be lonely here with just me.'

'But that's what you wanted initially. Are you saying you want me to take him with me?'

'No, no.' She took a little breath, trying not to tangle the little web of untruths she'd woven. 'It's just…is this the way it's going to be for ever? Are we going to live separately for ever? And what about if you meet someone else? What about if you fall in love with—?'

'I won't fall in love with anyone,' he said tightly. 'I told you that love wasn't a part of this.'

'Not with me, sure. But what if you—?'

'I won't.' His voice was terse and there was something glittering in his dark gaze that made her chest constrict.

She didn't want him to be in love with anyone else. The very thought made her want to cry, and yet now she'd broached the topic, she couldn't seem to shut herself up. 'You might want someone else,' she said. 'Yet you're married to me. I told you I didn't want to be bound by anyone's rules, but you're also being bound, aren't you?'

'That's true.' His gaze abruptly became very focused on her. 'But when I said I won't fall in love with anyone else, I meant it. I won't want anyone else either. There's only you, Maude.'

She swallowed, a lump in her throat. 'But...why?'

'You're beautiful, fascinating, mysterious. You're passionate about the things that are important to you and you're honest. You're brave.'

The words felt like stones being thrown at her and suddenly she couldn't bear it. He thought she was all these wonderful things and she wasn't any of them. She was just a silly little girl left standing by a car while people who didn't want her argued about who got lumped with her.

Also, she was a liar.

Maude pushed herself out of his arms, unable to bear being so close to him when he didn't know the truth about her, sliding off the couch and going to stand in front of the fireplace.

'Maude?' Dominic asked, his voice full of concern. 'What is it?'

She wrapped her arms around herself as she stared into the flames. 'I'm not honest,' she said bluntly. 'I've been lying to you this whole time.'

There was a silence behind her.

'About what?' he asked eventually.

Maude took a breath. If she was really as brave as

he thought she was, then she needed to face him. This was too important to tell the fire. He was too important.

Slowly, she turned around.

He hadn't moved from the couch, his expression unreadable, his dark eyes glittering.

Maude took her courage in both hands and held on. 'When I said I didn't love you, I lied.'

He said nothing, still staring at her.

'I've fallen in love with you, badger,' she said, the words falling into the silence like pebbles in a still pond, creating ripples. 'I know we said love wasn't a part of this, but… It's become part of it for me and I…' She swallowed, her throat aching. 'I don't want to be a millstone around your neck or drag you down. I know you didn't choose to have this baby or to have me as your wife. In fact, you didn't want a family at all. And I'm sorry that I put you into this position. I…just want you to know that, if you don't want any of this, if you want to walk away, I won't stop you. And I wouldn't blame you either.'

Dominic stared at Maude, standing with her back to the flames, her arms still wrapped around herself as if she were cold. She was in leggings and one of his sweatshirts, the dark green one, and it was giant on her, the hem extending down to her mid-thigh. Her hair was loose the way he liked it to be, in a wild golden storm down her back, and her face was flushed. She looked so beautiful, but what he didn't like was the anguish in her brown eyes.

Nor did he like the flood of words that had just come out of her mouth.

In fact, they'd shocked him.

Firstly, love. What the hell did she mean that she'd fallen in love with him? How? Why? He'd told her *specifically* that love wasn't a part of their marriage and yet that was exactly what she'd done.

Secondly, why the bloody hell would she assume that he'd happily walk away from their child and her if given the option? And now? After he'd married her?

He stared at her silently, his temper pulling at the leash.

The past week being married to her had been the happiest he'd ever known, and he'd indulged himself shamelessly. Going to her cottage every night and holding her in his arms. Then for the first time, a couple of days after their wedding, she'd turned up at the manor, apparently looking for him.

He'd allowed the fierce burst of satisfaction that had brought him, inviting her in for dinner, and then the same the next night, and the one after that. He was hoping to entice her eventually into sleeping with him, in his room, and he'd thought tonight she might actually allow it, and now… This.

She'd ruined it. She'd turned this magical little affair they were having into something it shouldn't be and all because of that hateful four-letter word. Love.

Love demanded and demanded. Love was a rigged game that couldn't be won no matter how hard you tried. Love locked you outside and left you terrified in the dark. Love called you weak and laughed at your pain.

Love was a canker that had to be cut out, a weakness, a vulnerability.

He didn't want it. He didn't need it. Not any more.

And as for the assumption that he'd walk away from his child...

'If you think,' he said finally, acidly, 'that I would walk away from my son now, after moving to Darkfell and insisting on marriage to you, then you have another think coming.'

She'd gone very pale. 'It's a business deal. That's what you said.'

'Yes, it was. So why are you now talking about love?' He was suddenly furious with her. 'You wanted your freedom, Maude, so I gave it to you. And I never insisted you be anyone other than who you were. You had the life you wanted, so why the hell would you want to change it?'

There were tears in her eyes, he could see them glittering in the light from the fire. 'I know,' she said thickly. 'I know I wanted all those things, and, yes, you gave them to me. But...that's why I fell in love with you. You're caring and you listen, and you've always accepted me. You've never wanted me to be someone I'm not. And when you make me promises you never break them.'

A tear ran down her cheek, sparkling in the light, and for some reason the sight of it felt like a knife in his heart. 'You're not really the man you seem to be on the outside. You're someone else deep down, someone who's as passionate as I am and cares as much as I do, and who feels like my soul mate. That's why I love you,

Dominic. You gave me everything I wanted. Except then I realised that what I really wanted was you.'

Dominic closed his eyes, not wanting to see her face or her tears.

He'd gone about this all wrong. He'd made a grievous mistake. He'd thought he could have his cake and eat it too, the way he always did. The way he'd done success-fully for years. Business and pleasure, yes, he could have both and did, frequently.

But marriage without love, a family without ties, was apparently *not* something he could have. Which meant he'd have to give something up, and that something would have to be her. There was no other option.

She loved him and he couldn't allow that. Wouldn't allow that. It would hurt her, and the thought of hurting her made him ache, but he'd been a fool to think that none of this would come without consequences.

He'd hoped that making this marriage a purely busi-ness proposition would keep love and all its ensuing pain out of it, yet apparently not.

What else could he do, though? Keeping her, as that deep, essential part of him kept growling, was not an option, not when he couldn't give her what she truly wanted: his heart.

It was frozen, that heart of his, and it wouldn't ever thaw. He didn't want it to. It was far better to keep it on ice, keep it out of other people's hands, because, after the way his father had treated him, he would never give anyone that kind of power over him again.

He had to let her go. It was the only way. Wasn't that

old saying 'if you love something set it free'? Trite and ridiculous, but that was the only way out of this.

So you'll actually do what she asked and walk away? From her? From your child?

The primitive part of him snarled in protest at the thought, but he crushed it. He couldn't walk away from his son, no, but he could walk away from Maude. He'd have to. Because that same primitive, possessive part of him was urging him to lie to her, to tell her that he loved her, then take her away to the city and keep her near him, and for always.

But he couldn't do that, either. He wouldn't be like her grandparents, taking her away from everything she loved, everything that was important to her, and surrounding her with concrete and metal. He would never take his wood nymph away from her trees.

As for his son…well, the child would be better living with Maude than with him. In fact, he couldn't think of anything better for his little boy than to grow up close to the natural world with Maude as his mother. She would love him, care for him. He'd never be lonely with her.

Dominic's chest ached at that thought, the pain of it lancing deep inside him, but he forced it away.

'Dominic? Say something, please.' She was still standing in front of the fire, tear tracks shining on her cheeks, her brown eyes full of anguish.

An anguish he was going to make worse, and he hated himself for it. But it was the only way.

He met her gaze. 'Say something?' he repeated. 'Say what?'

'I don't know. Anything.'

'Fine.' Slowly he rose from the couch. 'Then how about this? I won't take you away from your trees. But you're right, I didn't choose this life and I didn't choose you. So maybe it is time for me to walk away.'

Her eyes darkened with pain. 'I… Yes, okay. And… our son?'

It was the first time she'd said 'our son' and that hurt too, but, again, he ignored it. 'He can stay here with you.' He had to force out the words, even as the snarling beast inside him ripped at the bars of the cage he'd trapped it in. 'I would never take him away from you and I'd…like him to be taught to care for the forest.'

'You can stay,' she said abruptly. 'It's not fair that you should have to leave, because of me. It's your house. I can go, I don't have to—'

'No,' he interrupted immediately, his tone fierce. 'I'm not forcing you to leave your forest. It's yours.'

Her brown eyes were full of tears, the gold drowned beneath them. 'It's not mine. It's your home.'

It was and yet he'd never felt at home here. Not until she'd come.

And while she's here, you can never stay.

Of course, he couldn't. This house and its grounds would be off-limits for him for ever. The temptation she presented would be too great, and he'd manipulate her, use her for his own ends, and end up hurting her worse than he was doing now. And he just couldn't allow that.

'It was yours more than it ever was mine,' he said and when she opened her mouth to protest, he added, 'I'm not arguing, Maude. It will be my legacy to my son. Keep it. For him.'

She nodded, standing rigidly in front of the fire as another tear slid down her cheek. And he wanted to close the distance, wipe that tear away then pull her into his arms and make her forget all about love and how it could hurt, but he didn't.

Instead he said, 'I'll leave tonight. No point in drawing this out any longer than it needs to be.'

She looked so fragile standing there in his sweatshirt, holding herself so stiffly it was as if she was afraid one touch would shatter her.

His lovely nymph.

'I would keep you if I could,' he said finally, unable to stay silent in this last terrible moment. 'I don't want to let you go. But if anyone deserves to be loved, Maude, it's you, and if I can't, you need to find someone else who will.'

Another tear slid slowly down her cheek. 'I won't,' she said, and he could hear all the force of her strong, stubborn will behind the words. 'There won't be anyone else but you, badger.'

He'd had no idea this would hurt so much or even why it did, but there was no other option. Walking away was all he could do.

His heart felt as if it were burning away, leaving nothing but ash as, without another word, he turned and strode from the room.

Yet he didn't hesitate.

And she didn't call him back.

CHAPTER TWELVE

DOMINIC HAD BEEN gone a week and Maude was worse than miserable, she was broken-hearted. She dragged herself around the forest, but not even the trees could comfort her, not this time.

She knew she'd done the right thing. She knew. But that little selfish piece of her kept crying and crying because he'd gone. Because he'd done exactly what she'd told him to do and walked away from her, and now there'd be emptiness in her heart for ever.

A just punishment, really, for how she'd lied to him and for how she'd given him nothing, while he'd given her the world and everything in it.

It was only fair that he walked away and only fair that he couldn't love her back. He'd been clear right from the start about the kind of arrangement they'd had, and if she was the one wanting more, then she should have stopped it right in the beginning.

Except she hadn't known she'd even want more, not until it was too late.

Eventually, she called her Your Girl Friday friends in a video call, and told them what had happened, baring her heart in a flood of words that left everyone silent for at least five minutes afterwards.

'So,' Lyanna said at last. 'Let me get this straight. You slept with a strange man in the forest at a mid-summer bacchanal, found yourself pregnant with his baby, and then the strange man turned out to be your boss and one of the worst playboys in Europe. Then he asked you to be his wife and so you married him, and now he's gone, yes?'

'Yes,' Maude said, grabbing a tissue from the nearby box and dabbing at her eyes with it. 'That's pretty much it.'

'Well,' said Auggie, clearly miffed. 'You kept that very quiet.'

'Dominic Lancaster's midsummer bacchanal, hmm?' Irinka was all curiosity. 'And with Dominic Lancaster himself. Is he as good as everyone says he is?'

'He's better.' Maude blew her nose into her tissue. Then she took a deep breath. 'And I'm in love with him.'

There was a silence.

Irinka frowned—she had her background blurred so Maude couldn't tell where she was. 'You married the man, so how is being in love an issue?'

'Because our marriage was a business agreement,' Maude explained. 'It was for the baby. He told me love wouldn't be a part of it and I agreed. And then...' her chest ached '...I actually fell in love.'

'That was poor timing,' Lyanna muttered.

'Extremely poor,' Irinka added.

But Auggie, newly married to her own wonderful ex-playboy husband, only gave her a clear-eyed stare. 'So what are you doing about it, Maude?'

Maude stared back. 'What do you think I'm doing? I'm not crying for fun, and, before you say anything, it's not pregnancy hormones.'

'What I mean,' Auggie said patiently, 'is did you just let him go?'

'Of course, I let him go.' Maude pulled out another tissue. 'He had a terrible childhood and his father was basically the devil, and he was very clear he doesn't want love. In fact...' she swallowed as another bubble of anguish rose '...he walked away rather than stay with someone who loved him.'

Lyanna frowned. 'How could he not stay with you? You're pregnant with his child, for God's sake.'

'It's not his fault,' Maude said, instantly wanting to defend him. 'I'm the one who fell in love with him. And I...refused to compromise about certain things. He's... just such a wonderful man. Yes, he has his flaws, but he accepted me in a way no one else ever has.'

'Hey,' Auggie muttered, along with various protestations from Irinka and Lyanna. 'We accept you.'

'I know you do,' Maude said, thinking of Dominic standing in front of her, his dark eyes haunted as he told her he was giving her Darkfell, that it was hers more than it had ever been his. Giving up the last piece of himself to her. Telling her that he didn't want to let her go, but he had to, and then walking away.

Alone. He was so alone. At least she had her friends, but who did he have? Perhaps he had friends too, but she was sure there was no one who loved him the way she did, with every part of her.

'But I'm not sure he has anyone,' she said into the silence, her chest sore. 'I... I wish he could feel what it was like to be loved. Just once.'

'So?' Auggie said. 'Why don't you go show him?'

Maude took a breath. 'He told me that—'

'Oh, who cares what he told you?' Auggie interrupted impatiently, provoking startled looks from Irinka and Lyanna. 'Men say all kinds of stupid things that they don't really mean. You're a wonderful person, Maude, and you deserve happiness. If you love him, don't let him walk away. And don't accept whatever silly excuses he chooses to throw at you, either. You go after him and you tell him that you can't live without him.'

Everyone else fell silent.

Maude stared at her screen, feeling her friends' words echo in her soul.

He didn't love her and he wouldn't, he'd made that very plain. And yet, regardless of that small part of her that was desperate for his love and had been hurt terribly by him walking away, she couldn't bear the thought of being apart from him either.

But he's gone and he's not coming back.

Yes, he had, but that didn't mean she couldn't go after him. She didn't go to the city, she didn't like it, she never had, but she couldn't leave him there alone amongst all that metal and concrete and glass. His father had left him like that, had made him negotiate for everything he'd wanted, but she would never do the same. She'd go to him, tell him that she loved him still and then she'd find somewhere to stay. And if he didn't want her, then at least she'd be close by with their child.

She would be his little piece of home, a little piece of wild Darkfell, in the vast city.

'Sorry,' she said to her friends. 'I have to go. I need to find out how to organise myself a helicopter.'

Dominic sat in his London office wondering what the hell he was going to do now. He didn't want to do anything, that was the issue. A couple of months ago he would have thrown himself into a party and taken one, two, or three women to bed, but he'd lost his taste for partying.

He'd lost his taste for anything that wasn't Maude, and his future looked so bleak he almost couldn't stand it.

You threw it away. You loved her and you threw her away.

Maybe. Maybe this painful, aching feeling in his chest was love. He didn't know. His heart had been frozen for so long he'd forgotten what it felt like.

But no, he couldn't tell himself that. He knew. It was the same helpless pain he'd felt when the man who was supposed to be his father had laughed at his anguish over the stag. Had shrugged when he'd cried over the itemised list he'd been given, all the expenses laid out of his upbringing. His relationship with his father reduced to pounds and pence, to cold, hard money. Dominic had never been given anything freely. He'd always had to pay for it.

She gave you her love freely. She didn't want anything in return.

He sat back in his office chair, London at his back, and shut his eyes.

He didn't want to think about Maude and the tears on her cheeks, telling him that she'd fallen in love with him, anguish in her warm brown eyes. She hadn't asked to be loved in return. She hadn't asked for anything. It had been him that she had been concerned about, telling him that none of this had been his choice, not her, not their baby…

Pain sat in his heart, eating at him with sharp teeth.

You fool. You bloody fool.

Oh, he knew it. And it was poetic, almost, to finally know what he wanted in life, to finally understand his purpose, only for it to be out of his reach.

He loved her. He loved their baby. He wanted the future he'd been able to see for them both, living at Darkfell as a family.

But he couldn't have it. He couldn't bargain for it. He couldn't buy it, not this precious future. Because in doing so, he'd cheapen it, and he couldn't bear to do that.

So you're happy to hurt her instead?

His beautiful wood nymph, crying because she was in love with him, giving him freely what he'd never been given before.

And he couldn't take it. Because ultimately he was just like his father. Everything was about the deal. Everything was about money. About cold, hard cash and a cold, hard heart. There was no room for warmth or passion. No room for the living, breathing things of the forest. And no room for the little family that might have been his.

He would never sentence Maude to the kind of life he lived, and he wouldn't sentence his son to it, either. It would kill her, and it would kill him too.

You can change, you know. It's not too late.

Ah, but that was the kicker, wasn't it? He couldn't change, not now. He was too old for that kind of thing, had lived too much of his life in the boardrooms. His heart was nothing but a frozen lump in his chest and nothing was going to shock it back to life.

Just then, his intercom buzzed. 'Mr Lancaster?' his secretary said. 'You have a—wait! You can't go in there!'

At the same moment the doors to his office were pushed wide and a woman strode through them.

She was dressed in maternity jeans that still had mud clinging to the knees and his green sweatshirt that just about swallowed her. Her hair was loose in wild golden skeins down her back, and there appeared to be a leaf caught in it.

His frozen heart was still and quiet in his chest.

He couldn't move.

He couldn't breathe.

It was his wood nymph, come to the city.

She was carrying a bag and as she dumped it on the floor next to his desk, her nose wrinkled. 'I'm disappointed, badger,' she said flatly. 'I was expecting to find you in bed with lots of women. But here you are sulking in your den.'

He had to say something, he had to. 'Maude,' he managed, his voice full of gravel. 'What the hell are you doing here?'

'What does it look like?' She surveyed his office and then the view out of the windows. 'I want you to show me the city.'

He stared at her, his brain moving so very slowly. 'What?'

Her gaze came to his, a deep forest pool dappled with sunshine. 'I showed you my world. Now I've come to see yours.'

'But…but…' He stopped. He'd never been lost for words before, not since he was a child, and he just couldn't comprehend what she was doing here.

'I was an idiot,' Maude said. 'I let you walk away without a word and I've never regretted anything more. I was afraid, badger. I wasn't your choice, I told you that, and neither was our baby, and I didn't want to be a millstone around your neck the way I was with my mother and my grandparents, so I…gave you a way out.' Her chin lifted in that stubborn way. 'But I was wrong to let you walk away. I love you, Dominic Lancaster, and I've been miserable without you. You don't have to love me back. You don't have to do anything at all for me. But I can't bear not being near you, so I've decided to move here. I can have the baby here and we can—'

'No!' The word burst out of him without any conscious thought, and he was on his feet, his chair pushed

back so violently it lay overturned on the floor. And he was coming around the side of the desk to her, full of some fierce, burning emotion he couldn't quite comprehend.

But maybe he didn't need to comprehend it. Maybe he didn't need to think about it or analyse it. Maybe he simply needed to obey it and so he did.

Her eyes were shining as he put his hands on her hips and jerked her into his arms. 'Nymph...' His voice was so rough it was barely intelligible. *'Nymph...'* And then her mouth was beneath his, so warm and sweet with that delicious tartness he'd come to hunger for more than his own breath. And his hands were in the raw silk of her hair, holding on for dear life, as if he was afraid she'd disappear again.

He *was* afraid she'd disappear again.

He was afraid of that fierce, burning feeling inside him. Afraid of what it meant. Afraid to trust it. Afraid to trust her and the heart she'd given him on a silver platter. But that heart of hers was valiant, and strong, and generous, an unbreakable tether holding him fast. Coaxing a thaw in his own, making a wild rose suddenly bloom.

'I'm sorry,' he whispered against her mouth. 'I'm so sorry I walked away. I was a coward and a fool, and I have been for weeks. I should have trusted what we had that night in the forest. I should have accepted it for what it was.' He lifted his head and gazed down into her eyes. 'I'd never met you. I'd never even seen your face. But that didn't matter. You were my choice that night, Maude, and you're my choice now. You've been my choice all along. My entire life I've been struggling to find a purpose and now I've found it.' He slowly tightened his fingers in her hair, his heart a bed of wild roses. 'It's you, nymph. It's you and our son.'

She smiled, warm as the midsummer sun, her eyes full of tenderness. 'My forest god,' she murmured.

He kissed her again, unable to stop. 'I love you, Maude Lancaster,' he said against her mouth. 'I love you so much.'

She deepened the kiss, giving him a wordless answer that flooded him with heat and the most peculiar sensation that he had the odd feeling was joy.

A few endless moments later, he lifted his head, because, while he was desperate for her, even he had standards and taking her on his desk was not one of them.

'Let's go home,' he said. 'To Darkfell.'

But Maude shook her head. 'No. I told you. I want to see the city.'

'Stubborn nymph.' He kissed her again, already reassessing his standards and thinking that maybe he could lower them just this once. 'I hope you're not meaning now.'

The gold in her eyes glittered, a sure sign that she was going to dig in on this. 'Of course now. Don't sulk, badger.'

He sighed. 'Come on, then,' he said, reluctantly releasing her, yet keeping hold of her hand. 'If you insist.'

Maude's gaze became hotter and suddenly very wicked. 'Well… I suppose I could wait a little longer.'

But Dominic was already striding to the doors and

shutting them, and locking them for good measure. Then he strode back to where she stood, and kissed her hard, letting the flames take them both.

It was going to be interesting, this new life of his. Interesting in ways he couldn't even begin to contemplate. But one thing he was sure of.

He couldn't wait to get started.

EPILOGUE

IT WAS HOT, and she was sweating, and Maude couldn't wait any longer.

As soon as they reached the pool, she pulled off all her clothes, climbed onto the rocks under the waterfall and dived head first into the water.

It was cool and refreshing after the baking midsummer heat, and she gave a little internal sigh of pleasure as she touched the sandy bottom of the pool in greeting to the water spirits, before arrowing back to the surface.

Dominic had stopped by the edge of the pool and had taken off the backpack with Robin, their twelve-month-old, in it. He was sitting now on the grass, holding Robin while the little boy tried to grab the white stripe of his father's hair in a chubby fist.

Ever since he'd been born, he'd been fascinated with it. He'd been fascinated with his father too, and Dominic had been equally smitten. Watching him with their son was one of Maude's special joys.

There was joy, too, to be had in the projects that she and Dominic chose together to invest in. Eco projects and technology, mostly, because she'd decided that she didn't want to save just Darkfell forest, she wanted to save the world too.

Since she'd already saved one disreputable playboy and turned him into a respectable family man, she didn't think saving the world was entirely out of reach, and certainly not with him at her side.

After all, he'd tamed a wild forest nymph and turned her into a wife and mother, so fair was fair.

But that wasn't all they were.

Sometimes, on warm nights, when the moon was full and the forest spirits walked, they'd go out into the woods and become forest spirits themselves, the god and goddess, wild and free and passionate, on a bed of bracken.

As Maude surfaced, Dominic waved at her and so did Robin.

Really, there was no end to the joy of her life, and soon enough it was going to get even more joyous.

Maude put a light hand to her stomach and smiled.

It would be a little girl, she knew it.

Dominic was going to be so happy.

* * * * *

Were you blown away by Boss's Heir Demand?
*Then you're sure to enjoy the first instalment in
the Work Wives to Billionaires' Wives quartet*
Billionaire's Bride Bargain
by Millie Adams

*And check out these other stories from
Jackie Ashenden!*

A Vow to Redeem the Greek
Enemies at the Greek Altar
Spanish Marriage Solution
Italian Baby Shock
The Twins That Bind

Available now!